ABIDING

Living Life Abundantly

RYAN SHIEH

ISBN 979-8-88616-728-3 (hardcover)
ISBN 979-8-88616-729-0 (digital)

Christian Faith Publishing
832 Park Avenue
Meadville, PA 16335
www.christianfaithpublishing.com

Scripture taken from the New King James Version®. Copyright © 1982 by Thomas Nelson. Used by permission. All rights reserved.

All Bible references are from NKJV unless otherwise noted.

Printed in the United States of America

To Jesus Christ, my Lord and Savior, who changed my life,
You are so good and so full of grace and mercy.
All praise, King Jesus.
Let my life be a reflection of you.

CONTENTS

ENDORSEMENTS

Abiding has the unique ability to tap into real struggles that we face every day in our walks with the Lord, while highlighting biblical solutions. Not only does *Abiding* hit every one of us right where we're at, but you can't go more than a paragraph without scriptural support to solidify each theme. It's a difficult task to write supplementally to the greatest book the world has ever known, but *Abiding* stays true to biblical doctrine and is very evidently Spirit-led in the words written; I believe it will be a great encouragement to all who read it.

—*Ryan Metz*
Virginia Tech Baseball (2018–2022)
Host of *The Christian Athlete Paradox* podcast

The meaning of true intimacy with Christ has been lost in our generation and culture today. So many carry the tragic misunderstanding that God's love and acceptance is something that we must work for or even earn. This is why I am so thankful for Ryan Shieh and his heart to write *Abiding*, which describes the process of developing true intimacy with God. In this book, you will learn what it means to abide in Christ so that you may experience the abundant life he has always desired for you. My friends, it is time to stop playing the religion card and, instead, start growing in a relationship with him.

—Zach Clinton
President and host
Ignite Men's Impact Weekend and the *Built Different Podcast*

ACKNOWLEDGMENTS

Without question, this book is not made possible without the presence and the power of the Holy Spirit and my Lord and Savior, Christ Jesus. All praise to him who was and is and is to come.

Holy Spirit, come.

To my publishers, editors, and assistants at Christian Faith Publishing, thank you all for your help and contributions to making this possible. I can't express how grateful I am for our partnership, and I look forward to more works in the future.

To my mom, none of these books would be done without your help and your support. From the bottom of my heart, thank you for your love, your assistance, and your willingness to serve me. You are so kind and always put me first, and it doesn't go unnoticed. I love you, Mom.

To my dad and brother, David, my two best friends, thank you both for the love you give me every single day. Dad, your support and guidance on my life is unmatched, and words can't express how grateful I am to be your son. David, I wouldn't want anyone else in this world to be my brother. You're such a light for the gospel, and I'm so proud of you. I love you both beyond words.

To Willa Grace, thank you for being such a vessel for the Spirit to work. Only me and you know, but this book would not have been written without you. You support me and challenge me to keep my priorities straight and be a better man. I love you and can't wait to serve Jesus with you for years to come.

To Zach Clinton, you are such a light in my life. Your words, your actions, your motives—everything you do points to Jesus. Thank you so much for helping me with this brother. I can't wait to grow with you over these next few years and look forward to seeing how God uses you in huge ways.

To Ryan Metz, thank you so much for your help in this! You have been a reflection of Jesus ever since we first met, and you do such a great job carrying your cross. Brother for life. Hope to see you soon! Love.

To everyone else in my life who has impacted me over the course of this project, thank you. You are so appreciated. Everyone at Liberty University, everyone involved in Liberty baseball, all the LU athletics assistants, and my friends, family, mentors, pastors, teachers, spiritual leaders, grandparents, teammates, coaches—I thank you all from the bottom of my heart.

Oh, and Oasis room 104. I love you all. My dudes for life.

INTRODUCTION

Knocking on the Door

There's got to be more.

One afternoon, as I just finished writing *Restart,* a previous book I had written, I sat at my desk and wondered, *There's got to be more. More love. More intimacy. More faith. More Jesus.*

Ever since I was a kid, I've grown up in the church. I went every Sunday, participated in all the activities they had, went to vacation Bible school every summer—you name it. I was *surrounded* by God—but had no idea who he was.

Fast-forward—senior year of high school. After a long break because of the COVID-19 pandemic, I finally had time to understand (kind of) what it meant to be a follower of Christ. "Jesus died for your sins. God is good. You're a representative of him with whatever you do, so do it well. And while you're at it, try to get as many people into the kingdom as you can."

Which, if you look at it from that perspective, is all fine and dandy.

But there was—more.

After finally finishing a book *about* God, I decided to actually *read* about who God is. Like *really* read—something I had never done before. The most reading I had ever done at that time was reading the road signs on the highway, and I still couldn't get home on my own! This was something brand-new to me. But I felt deeply convicted to slow down and actually meet and encounter God.

So I read.

And read.

And read.

And after a little over a year, I read through the entire Bible. For the first time in my life, I read all about God's time line, God's will, and God's plan for redemption. It was right there for my own access. The Bible isn't something you just take from and apply to your life. The Bible is God's living Word that gives you the completeness of his character. It's used for knowing Jesus, not bettering your morals. And after reading about creation from God's point of view, I concluded something that we don't hear very often: *there is so much more.*

Those words bring me so much joy. Let's be honest. Chances are if you're reading this book, you are a Christian who knows about Jesus. At some point in your life, you were introduced to him at the perfect time in the perfect place, and you haven't looked back. You got saved, you accepted Christ as Lord and Savior, and from then on, when people ask about your spirituality, you call yourself a follower of Jesus.

But it doesn't stop there. You begin to actually pray a little bit. You start to listen to worship songs, and you memorize *all* the lyrics. You get the very last spot in the parking lot (closest to the entrance of course), and you are fully convinced that it was God's hand working in your life. Life is good. And because life is good, you conclude God is good.

But then—the initial excitement starts to fade away. You begin to recognize again that we still live in a broken world. We still have responsibilities to take care of. We still have problems. And after trial and tribulation, you begin to walk away from your faith because what you *see* in the moment has brought you to a conclusion that God is simply not as good as you thought he was.

Why? Here's the problem: we don't *know* God. We know *of* him—but we don't *know* him.

What? What do you mean? I go to church. I sing the songs. I even have a verse in my Instagram bio! I know God. Don't you ever accuse me of anything otherwise.

But if you looked at the way we lived our lives, we could say something much different. And it's not even the sin that tells the story—it's everything. The choices we make. The decisions we follow through with. The way we love. The way we speak. The way we handle situations. What we choose to do with our time. It all comes back to the same question—do we *really* know God?

Maybe today, you're wondering this for yourself, *Do I really know Jesus? I mean, I want to have a good relationship with him, but I don't even know how. Where do I start? What do I do? Will my efforts ever be enough?* And because we don't know how to get close to Jesus (which is a common drawback), we simply give up and forget to even try. We settle for something less than what God originally intended for us to have: intimacy.

There's got to be more.

And there is. After finally reading through the entire Bible, Old and New Testament, I saw how God clearly conveys his most important desire with his people. God wants a *relationship* with you. That's it. He doesn't want your works, your good efforts, your morals, or anything else you can think of that can earn you favor. God doesn't want your *religion.* He wants your heart.

Maybe this sounds like you. You're a Christian, who's been saved, but you ask yourself the same question as I did. Is there more? Is there more to this whole Jesus thing than just going to church on Sundays? Is there more we aren't experiencing because we settle for something less? Is there a deeper life Jesus is inviting us to that we don't even recognize?

Is there something we're missing?

The answer? Yes. There is *so* much more than what we think. More love. More freedom. More intimacy. More direction. More goodness. More faithfulness. More connection. More of a relationship.

There's more to this whole Jesus thing than just religion.

Jesus Holds More

Jesus said in John 10:10, "I have come that they may have life, and that they may have it more abundantly" (NKJV). Obviously, we see here that the life Jesus is inviting us to holds more, bringing something divine. The word for *abundantly* in Greek, used here, is *perissos,* which means "far greater, excessive, or exceeding than what you can think of." Jesus is waiting to show you this brand-new life full of overwhelming love, never-ending joy, and indescribable intimacy.

But you have to want it.

Notice—finding Jesus doesn't come by *working* for it. It's by simply *wanting* it. It's a free choice, not something you have to earn your way toward. James 4:8 says, "Draw near to God and He will draw near to you." It's a *relationship*. A relationship is always formed by love, not by works.

John 15:4 says, "Abide in Me, and I in you. As the branch cannot bear fruit of itself, unless it abides in the vine, neither can you, unless you abide in Me." Famous evangelist Dr. Tony Evans is quoted by saying, "Jesus doesn't want you to just learn about him, study some stories, post some scripture, and throw up some prayers. He wants a relationship with *you*. That's the kingdom encounter you need to pursue. It's called abiding." The Greek word for *abide* used in John 15 is *menó*, which means "to remain or stay with."

Abiding with Jesus isn't trying to impress him. Abiding with Jesus is being as close to him as you can. It's not about behavior—it's about love.

That's all he ever wanted—a relationship. One that is built on his love, his grace, and his mercy. *That's* the *more* we're going to get into. And I promise, if you seek him diligently and long for his heart, you will come out on the other side with the intimacy and the presence you want.

That's a satisfaction guarantee, not from me but from Jesus himself (Revelation 3:20).

As you read, I challenge you. I challenge you to open your heart and listen to the Spirit. Prioritize obedience. Because the more you can listen to *him* and not just my words, the more you will be divinely directed to conform to his will and his way.

Is intimacy with Jesus something that just happens? Long story short, no—not a chance. Relationships take work. But the good news is, when you look at life from a perspective of purpose, you see how every action, every outcome, and every scenario point you back to Jesus and the cross. We're going to walk through everything Jesus has shown me over the last year and a half, and I pray that he speaks to you in a big way because, truthfully, I've experienced both sides of the spectrum—full of his presence and lacking it completely. And that's why it is so important to talk about such a matter like this one.

I am nowhere near perfect, and I'm not a religious guy by any means, but I do know Jesus, not because I've earned it but because I know he died in my place and, somehow, wants a relationship with me. Do I deserve it? No. Not a chance. But grace in itself is what draws me closer to him.

Are you ready? I am. It's time to unlock life but, this time, life sponsored by Jesus—abundance. He is inviting you into a deeper walk full of peace, rest, surrender, and direction.

There's more to this whole Jesus thing than just checking boxes because Jesus doesn't want your efforts or your appeals. He just wants a relationship with you.

He's been waiting all along.

CHAPTER 1

Goodbye Religion

Houston, We Have a Problem—

My family loves to travel.

Ever since I can remember, my family and I have always traveled. Whether it was a baseball trip, a family gathering, or even just a vacation, we always were on the go. And if your family is anything like mine, we like to keep memories. We take pictures, capture videos, keep souvenirs—all so we can remember the good times again in years to come.

Most of these memories? Good. Being together and embracing each other while seeing what's going on around the world is super cool. But there is one story we always fall back on from a vacation, and although it's funny now, in the moment, it wasn't very funny at all.

This story is about me.

When I was about five or six, my family and I took a trip to Florida. As a young kid, I was blown away. It was my first time away from home, and I got to experience the beautiful Florida beaches, as well as seeing killer whales up close at *SeaWorld*. But the most memorable spot of that trip was a go-cart track on the side of the main strip, where I would do something that would never be forgotten.

As I walked up to the track, I noticed very quickly that nobody was in line in front of me and nobody was currently driving a car around. I had the entire track to myself! So I suited up, picked out a car, and got rolling. I drove as fast as I could around every turn, and as I completed each lap, I looked up at my dad to see if I was driving like a professional race car driver. Sure enough, I was.

But then, the worst possible thing happened. After all the fun I already had, speeding around the track, I looked up to see my worst nightmare. Something I never, ever wanted to see at that go-cart track. Something so unheard of it's hard for me to even write about.

Somebody else got in line.

To my disgust, I watched this new person walk up to the line and immediately jump into a car. And soon enough, they were drifting out on the course with me. I began to think, *It'll be all right. They'll stay out of your way. Not a big deal. This is still your track. Zoom on.*

But they didn't stop. They actually went *faster.* They were driving in my lane, in my direction, and on my track. And six-year-old me was not very happy.

So what happened? I did what every six-year-old Christian would do. I politely let her pass and made sure she took every lap very carefully. I drove side by side with her, making sure she wouldn't hit a rail. I waved her on so there wouldn't be any confusion. And at the end of our time, when we got out of the carts, I presented the gospel to her.

I wish I could say that's true, but that's not what happened. She started driving, and the moment I got close to her car, I rammed into her backside and spun her front tires around as she hit a bumper *and* got stuck. She started crying. The attendant came to help her, and I sped along after claiming territory once again to my track.

Without hesitation, I made the decision that seemed most beneficial to me. I got her off the track. Selfishly, without even thinking, I chose to ram into her because what I wanted mattered most. I didn't care about other people. I just cared for myself.

Where did I get this self-centered thinking from? Did my parents teach it to me? Did I learn it from the Internet? No. The fact of the matter is, we are *sinful people.* Romans 3:10–12 says:

> There is none righteous, no, not one; there
> is none who understands; there is none who seeks
> after God. They have all turned aside; they have
> together become unprofitable; there is none who
> does good, no, not one.

In order to clearly embrace the goodness of God, you must acknowledge the severity of your sin because we will never fully appreciate the necessity of a Savior until we see the extremity of our sin.

Jesus said in Mark 2:17, "Those who are well have no need of a physician, but those who are sick. I did not come to call the righteous, but sinners, to repentance." If we weren't sick, we wouldn't feel the *need* for a doctor. And in the same way, if we don't understand our sin, we won't see the need for a Savior.

You never fully see the need for Jesus until you recognize you are in need of saving.

The Good Doctor

So many Christians today think that the only way to get to God is to be a good person. Without any sort of evidence to support it, we claim that God *only* wants our good works and heaven is *only* full of morally good people.

But if you read any page in the Bible, you will find out that's totally not the case. Because reality is—we *all* have fallen short of the glory of God (Romans 3:23). There is no one righteous and no one good enough to make it to heaven. By our own efforts, if we were to approach the kingdom and tell God we lived good enough lives to be counted as righteous, we would be denied.

God is holy, and anything unholy cannot be in his perfect presence. We, as people, are *unholy.* We *cannot* be in his presence! There isn't some scale out there that measures the good and bad and, if your good outweighs the bad, you can make it into heaven. No. You by yourself will *never* be good enough to be in God's presence because of your sin.

Never. You can assist millions of people. You can give thousands of dollars to the poor. You can help kids, serve others, make a difference, you name it. But bottom line is, without Jesus, you and I are still the same sinners as we've always been. You and I are *not* good people. Welcome to this book, where the main goal is to make you feel better about yourself.

That was just a little joke. But truth be told, this is a point we must understand. We are in no way eligible to attain eternity; we simply aren't good enough. But the good news is, you don't *have* to be good enough—because Jesus is enough.

Sure. Everyone knows the story of the cross. Jesus died and rose again, *blah blah blah*. But to *really* understand and appreciate what he did, you must accept the human condition. We are without hope, without light, without any sort of chance to be good enough for God. But in his mercy, Jesus came to pay our price and cover our wage.

There is no possible way you can be spiritually dead if you understand that. Grace isn't a do-it-yourself project. Grace is a completely free gift from God. *I am a sinner, a pretty good one to say the least. And I am nowhere close to being good enough to be right in God's eyes. But because of what Jesus did on that cross, I am completely forgiven and redeemed of my sin. I am loved, chosen, and now counted as righteous because of what he did for me.*

That should spark insurmountable joy, not because it's a feel-good message but because the fact of the matter is, we have been purchased for freedom by the blood of Jesus.

You only appreciate Jesus as much as he deserves when you acknowledge the severity of your sin. And when you do embrace his grace, you should be directly pointed toward righteous joy.

Relationship Restored

So if that's the case, we can see clearly how badly God desires a relationship with you. Does he *need* it? No. God is perfect and completely fine all by himself.

But does he *want it?*

Absolutely yes. God *really* wants a relationship with you.

Just look at what he did. He bankrupted heaven and sent his only Son without knowing if we would love him or not. He took the chance and went out on a loop, not because he was promised love in return but because he loved us enough to offer it anyway. *That's* who our God is. John 3:16 says, "For God so loved the world that He gave His only begotten Son, that whoever believes in Him should not perish but have everlasting life." Notice the wording used here. God sent his *only* Son to save the world. Why? Because God *loved* the world. It doesn't say God hated the world so he sent his Son and had no other choice. God loved us so much he became man in Jesus, walking in the same dirt as you and me, not because he wants us to be perfect but because he wants to know and love you in a deeper, intimate way.

He wants your heart.

Go back to the very beginning. What did God want with Adam and Eve in the garden? To *walk* with them, to surround them, for them to be in his presence and experience his goodness. That's all he ever wanted. But so often, we are pounded with this idea that he wants something else.

Why? Because we see God as a demanding judge, not a loving Father. We think we have to prove it to him by our good works and behavior in order for us to have a relationship. We connect seeking him for intimacy with calling on him for salvation, which confuses the entire point of the gospel.

Understand this point: there is *nothing* you can do to earn favor with God. Nothing. Not good works, spotless behavior, perfect morals, nothing. There isn't a single thing you can do to earn favor with God because it's all given freely through the death and resurrection of Jesus Christ. Will you seek him more after you embrace grace? Yes. Absolutely. Your appreciation for grace should ignite a flame inside you to seek him. But first and foremost, you are always counted as righteous because of Jesus, not yourself.

So what does God want? God wants intimacy, closeness, a deep relationship built off his goodness and his faithfulness. He is providing it all for you. Look at these scriptures and see how God values relationship over religion:

> For I desire mercy and not sacrifice, and the knowledge of God more than burnt offerings. (Hosea 6:6)

> With what shall I come before the Lord, and bow myself before the High God? Shall I come before Him with burnt offerings, with calves a year old? Will the Lord be pleased with thousands of rams, ten thousand rivers of oil? Shall I give my firstborn for my transgression, the fruit of my body for the sin of my soul? He has shown you, O man, what is good; and what does the Lord require of you but to do justly, to love mercy, and to walk humbly with your God? (Micah 6:6–8)

See the perspective these Israelites are coming from? After years and years of idolatry and sin, they finally (for a moment) came back to God in hopes of making it up to him. And they asked themselves questions: What should we do? How much do you think he wants? What can we all sacrifice to him to prove that we are good again? What can we give to earn his favor?

Do we not do the same thing today?

"You search the Scriptures, for in them you think you have eternal life; and these are they which testify of Me. But you are not willing to come to Me that you may have life" (John 5:39–40).

Sure, you search the scriptures all day, but they don't contain eternal life! We try to find *other* ways of getting to God besides Christ.

Instead of receiving love through the grace of the Father, we try to *work* our way there through other things—things that aren't *Jesus*.

Maybe if I just read my Bible again today, God will love me, or if I go to church this week, maybe that'll mean God will show up again in my life—or maybe if I give or maybe if I serve or maybe if I love someone, or maybe…or maybe…or maybe…

Or maybe if I just do something in my *own* efforts, God will love me.

But God says no. That's not what he wants. What did he require of the Israelites? To do what is right, love mercy, and walk humbly with him. That's it. God could've told them to give him as many offerings as the world has ever seen! But he prioritizes intent of the heart over an act of righteousness, just to put on a show. God didn't want the Israelites' material goods. He wanted their *heart*.

And he wants yours too. Because ever since the beginning, what God wants more than anything is just a deep relationship with you. The God of the universe wants to know *you* and walk with *you* intimately. Do we deserve it? Not a chance! But that in itself should draw us closer to him.

God never wanted perfection. He wants a genuine, heartfelt repentance with a longing desire to know him intimately and walk with him faithfully.

Does this mean we can sin whenever we want? Of course not. Romans 6:1–2 says, "What shall we say then? Shall we continue in sin that grace may abound? Certainly not! How shall we who died to sin live any longer in it?" Can we just sin whenever we want? Of course not. But the fact of the matter is God will always prioritize repentance over perfection.

How can we tell? Scripture gives the whole story. Let's look at two different encounters from two different stories—Jesus speaking to a woman caught in adultery, and Jesus speaking to the Pharisees.

The Pharisees were the religious leaders of the day. They practically *lived* to scold people about how they didn't live perfectly; they were extreme hypocrites. But do you think Jesus was happy with them, even though they claimed to obey every law? Not a shot.

> Woe to you, scribes and Pharisees, hypocrites! For you are like whitewashed tombs which indeed appear beautiful outwardly, but inside are full of dead men's bones and all uncleanness. Even so you also outwardly appear righteous to men, but inside you are full of hypocrisy and lawlessness. Serpents, brood of vipers! How can you escape the condemnation of hell? (Matthew 23:27–28, 33)

What? My sweet little Jesus is actually calling someone a hypocrite? Now let's look at what Jesus said to the adulterous woman. She was caught by the Pharisees in her own sin and had no way of justifying it. But she was genuinely repentant and genuinely wanted change. And Jesus said this:

> "Woman, where are those accusers of yours? Has no one condemned you?" She said, "No one, Lord." And Jesus said to her, "Neither do I condemn you; go and sin no more." (John 8:10–11)

Jesus, to the *sinner,* said, "I don't condemn you." But to the religious leaders who claimed perfection, he said, "Woe to you." He called them hypocrites.

Notice the difference. To the ones who claimed to be *perfected* in the law, Jesus said, "You will be condemned to hell!" But to the woman who genuinely wanted a turnaround, he said, "I don't condemn you. Go and sin no more."

How can it be that different? Because of the same point, we keep highlighting: God does not require nor expect perfect behavior. He simply wants a willingness to change and a faithful heart of obedience.

Because God never asked for perfection; he just wants change—a real longing to be different, a genuine repentance that brings you closer to real intimacy with him.

After all the sin in my life, somehow, God still wants me. And the good news is, God doesn't want me to try to make up for it with good works. He simply wants me to love him.

God just wants my heart.

Not Religion, Just Jesus

As a freshman baseball player at Liberty University, I was encouraged to go to a three-week bridge program over the summer, on campus, to get accustomed to college life. Along with many other athletes from all different sports, I would go and meet my new friends (eventually my teammates), see how the baseball program operates, and find my way around campus. So right after my senior year of high school, I drove down to Liberty, ready to take on three weeks of my first time away from home by myself.

And it didn't disappoint. I met some of my best friends there, along with seeing this new way of life at Liberty. Life was definitely different, but with so much time came a lot of opportunities to seek after God and build relationships with new people.

It also warranted opportunities to get into some trouble.

And as I got a hold of this brand-new freedom, away from any sense of discipline, I was surrounded by sin on all sides, needing to decide what I was going to do. So me, being Mr. Christian, decided there was no way I was going to get into trouble. My religion tells me not to do it, so I'm not going to do it. With my good behavior, I thought I was actually pleasing God and earning my way to more love and more righteousness, which, if you haven't already figured out, was incorrect.

During those three weeks, I did not spend a lot of time in the Word or in prayer or in worship. The only thing I did was behave well! And because I thought my good behavior could earn my way to the Father, I substituted seeking God for intimacy with *pleasing* God for favor. I figured, as long as I behaved well, I wouldn't lose this intimate relationship I had with the Lord.

But truth be told—I was wrong. Reality was, during those three weeks of spotless behavior against temptations, I felt farther from

God than I ever had before, not because I had sinned but because there was no genuine seeking of him and his presence. I was so confused because I thought I had it all right. But the truth of the matter is this:

Intimacy doesn't come from good works. Intimacy comes from a deep, relational connection.

Religion is an outward gesture in hope that other people see we are right with God. It's our efforts and attempts to prove that we are good enough and we have checked the boxes. But the life and walk with Jesus you long for doesn't come from good works or good behavior. That next step we're talking about won't just appear the better you behave. It comes when you relationally get to know Jesus as your friend and Savior. Remember, God never wanted your perfection. Through knowing Christ as Lord, he wants your heart. And Jesus said that "no one can come to the Father but through Me" (John 14:6).

The problem? We aren't the only ones fighting this battle. On top of our own thoughts and ways, we have an enemy roaring around like a lion, looking for someone to devour (1 Peter 5:8). If Satan can get you to connect your identity to your behavior, he has already won—because if you see your relationship with God as something you have to *work* for you are completely losing sight of grace.

The enemy wants to define you by your shame. But Jesus wants to define you by his scars.

That's where your identity comes from—from him! You don't lose love or favor when you slip up because your identity was never based upon your own behavior. It always goes back to the cross. And the more you remember your identity comes from Christ, the more you will realize none of your own efforts can contribute to it.

Second Corinthians 5:17 says, "Therefore, if anyone is in Christ, they are a new creation; old things have passed away; behold, all things have become new." If you are *in* Christ, you are brand-new. The old is gone, and the new is here. You are no longer defined by your shame, your sin, your guilt, your disappointment.

Point-blank, you are no longer defined by you. You are defined by exactly who he says you are.

How can it be? Because God is gracious. And in his rich mercy, while we were dead in sin, he made us alive together with Christ (Ephesians 2:4–6). See, when you become a Christian and accept Christ as Lord, your efforts are no longer important. You're saved by grace, not by works (Ephesians 2:8–9). And there is no more condemnation for those who are in Christ Jesus (Romans 8:1). You are a brand-new creation with a brand-new life, with a brand-new goal: intimacy with Jesus.

Your priority isn't to make him proud. Your priority is to *know* him as deeply as you can! Because remember, God never wanted your efforts of perfection; he wants your heart.

You know who you are when you remember whose you are. I'm not who I once was. I am Christ's. And whatever he says, I believe.

Paul in the New Testament understood this beautiful concept. He says in Galatians 2:16:

> Knowing that a man is not justified by the works of the law but by faith in Jesus Christ, even we have believed in Christ Jesus, that we might be justified by faith in Christ and not by the works of the law; for by the works of the law no flesh shall be justified.

See, Paul finally had his chains broken. He says all the good works he did are *worthless* compared to just *knowing* Christ with infinite value (Philippians 3:8). After seeing Jesus and converting into a Christ follower, Paul finally understood that his behavior couldn't affect the way God sees him. Since Paul was *in* Christ—that was enough.

Jesus was enough.

Paul later said this in Galatians 2:19, "For I through the law died to the law that I might live to God." Paul says when he *tried* to be perfect, he failed because he was still the same sinner in need of saving. But then, he realized the main concept all along: God wants intimacy, not works. So Paul died to the law and no longer lived trying to be perfect. And what did that do in effect? It caused him to live for God.

Because Paul understood his identity. If he is in Christ, his identity is Christ. Jesus *was* Paul's literal identification. And after giving up, trying to impress Jesus, that's where he found true intimacy.

No matter where you are today or where you feel like you stand with God, let this be a freedom. The entire time, God never wanted you to feel like you have to earn your way there. He just wants you to seek him, and he'll meet you in the middle.

The good news? He promises to pick you up—*every single time.*

Surrounded

Maybe up to this point, you feel like you're in a gray area. You kind of understand everything we've talked about, but you don't think it applies to you. You're too far gone. You've done too much in your past. There's no way God still loves you. And you might feel like, after all your efforts of trying to make it up to God again and you *still* don't know him like you want to—it might be time to give up.

I'm here to tell you otherwise. Because no matter how far you've run, God hasn't gone anywhere. He has *surrounded* you the entire time, continually protecting and providing for you and your life. Romans 8:38–39 says:

> For I am persuaded that neither death nor life, nor angels nor principalities nor powers, nor things present or things to come, nor height nor death, nor any other created thing, shall be able to separate us from the love of God which is in Christ Jesus our Lord.

You know what *nothing* means in Greek and Hebrew? It means *nothing.* There is nothing that can separate you from the love of God, and through this next story, we are going to see the power of the presence of the Lord Almighty through a name you may not have heard before: Elisha.

Elisha was an Old Testament prophet who, after Elijah, did most of God's work throughout 2 Kings. Elisha was a faithful man, and he did many signs and wonders that showed the power of the work of God in him. But this one particular story in 2 Kings 6 is so incredibly powerful that I felt guilty if I didn't include it in this book. Pay attention to the characters' circumstances and emotions here, as well as their shift in perspective.

During this time, Aram was at war with Israel. And in 2 Kings 6:8, we see that the king of Aram would discuss with his officers on where he wanted to mobilize his troops. Like any good leader in battle, putting certain troops in certain places (at certain times) could have a big effect on how the outcome of the battle goes. The only problem was, Israel was God's chosen people—and God was fighting for them, not Aram. So God spoke to Elisha and told him exactly where the enemy troops were going (v. 9).

But this didn't just happen one time. Scripture says this happened "time and time again" (v. 10). Imagine, you are the king of Aram. You're trying to make a dent in Israel during this war, but every time you make a plan, someone finds out about it. Pretty frustrating! And the king was not happy. After hearing it was Elisha, the king decided he wanted to seize him. So he set out to capture Elisha, who was hiding out at Dothan.

But the king didn't just politely seize him. The king *really* wanted him captured, and he sent an entire military fleet to surround the place where Elisha was staying. And out of fear, Elisha's servant asked, "What shall we do?" (v. 15).

> So he answered, "Do not fear, for those who are with us are more than those who are with them." And Elisha prayed, and said, "Lord, I pray, open his eyes that he may see." Then the Lord opened the eyes of the young man, and he saw. And behold, the mountain was full of horses and chariots of fire all around Elisha. (vv. 16–17)

Don't be afraid. Because although the enemy has an army surrounding us—we have the Lord God surrounding them. With heavenly horses and chariots of fire, God was already there. He never left. And in the face of adversity, he was everything they needed, exactly when they needed it.

Open your eyes! See what the Lord is doing. Because you are never alone and never too far. He is there. He will never leave you nor forsake you (Hebrews 13:5). And you are completely under the direction and provision of the Lord our God.

No matter where you are or how far you run, you are always surrounded by God and his presence.

Let this be an encouragement to you. It's not too late. You can *still* have the intimacy you want with Jesus Christ. And as we continue, I pray that the Spirit speaks to you in a big way. Because Jesus is practically knocking at your door, asking if he can come in (Revelation 3:20). And through the power of the gospel, this relationship with him can be renewed, restored, and reborn. But it starts with understanding identity and God's will for your life.

God wants a relationship with you. He has already surrounded you from the beginning, and through his Son, he wants to know and lead you in a deep, intimate way.

And the catch is—you don't have to earn any of it because his love and grace are free gifts.

You just have to *want* him.

CHAPTER 2

Relationship Building

Building Your Foundation

Okay, cool. So I can sin whenever I want to, and God will still love me the same. God doesn't necessarily want my perfection, so I guess he doesn't care about how I live.

This is the balance we must find when understanding what God desires. God wanting our hearts is not an excuse to sin, rather we give him our hearts because we find what he offers is *better* than sin—more love, more peace, more joy, more purity, more life. That's why it's called a *relationship*. Relationships are built on intentional choices of love.

Think about it this way. Let's say one of your best friends asks you to write a review on them for a job interview. Obviously, they really want this job, and your words could be the gateway they need to launch their new career. And since they're your best friend, you want what's best for them. What do you do? You put extreme thought and consideration into what you're writing and make sure it is your top priority to honor your friend with good words. You want this job for them too! So you do your very best with no excuses.

But what if a random stranger came up to you and asked you to write a review on them for a possible job? What if someone, who you didn't know and didn't care as much about, asked you to do something for them? If in any way you're a human being, the natural response wouldn't be as interested or invested. Not only do you not know this person, but the *relationship* is not there. Sure, you might put some nice words simply based on their appearance, but the thought, care, and intent wouldn't be as strong as it would for someone you truly care about.

It's the same way with God. We should be so overwhelmed by God's goodness and love that we *want* to honor him. Jesus said in John 14:15, "If you love Me, keep My commandments." This cause and effect is the basis of the entire Christian faith. The more you grow a love for God, the more longing for obedience you will have. Remember, it's a *relationship.* When you look at him as your friend and Savior, you should *desire* to honor him because his goodness warrants it.

If you have truly understood grace, the overwhelming gratitude you get will be what leads and drives you to do certain things and make certain choices. It's a reaction based on what you have received. "God has been so good to me that I *want* to follow him. He gives me a love and grace I do not deserve, and because he is that good, he is worthy of my praise. I am choosing to honor him because he freely loves me."

Boom. Relationship. Something religion doesn't offer.

But the problem is, we don't see it that way. We don't see God as our friend. We see him as someone who only wants to judge us, and if we aren't too careful, he'll turn away. But the fact of the matter is, relationships aren't built on what you do for someone but on how much you *value* them. If you truly love God, you will have a longing, desire to keep his commandments, not because you have to but because you *want* to.

Okay. Jesus is my friend. He wants a relationship with me. But how? How do I do it? Does it just happen? What should I do to grow in my relationship with Jesus?

I can promise you this: you will never, ever just happen to somehow have a relationship with Jesus.

You will never wake up one random morning and say, "Wow! I feel closer to Jesus today!" Never. Seeking Jesus doesn't just happen.

It is a series of choices and decisions to seek after him and long for his presence.

Now, don't confuse this. You are not working for your relationship. You are *building* it. Salvation comes from grace, but intimacy comes from seeking. You aren't qualifying for religion but, instead, bettering a relationship. See it from a viewpoint of you are trying to know Jesus better, not impress him more.

Scripture promises that if we seek him with all our heart, we will surely find him (Jeremiah 29:13). Scripture also says that if we draw near to God, he will draw near to us (James 4:8). Do you see? God wants a relationship, but he will never force you. But if you willingly seek him with all your heart and so long for this intimate life with him, he will show up. That's a promise!

How? Here are three things you can do to increase intimacy with the Lord:

1. *Reading Your Bible*

   It sounds so easy, doesn't it? But reality is, reading Scripture is one of the hardest things for us to do. The number one thing, over anything else, that will increase intimacy with God is reading his Word. You want to hear God's voice? It's right here! God's Word is living water (John 7:37–39). His Word is alive and sharper than a double-edged sword (Hebrews 4:12). His Word is your only offensive weapon against the wiles of the devil (Ephesians 6:17). And his Word is *literally* God breathed (2 Timothy 3:16). His Word is powerful. And even when you don't feel it, maybe God will speak to you, through his Word, something you would never have otherwise received.

2. *Prayer*

   What is prayer? Prayer is a direct way of communication and the only source of dialogue between you and God. Prayer is a way for you to specifically give God the cries of your heart and worries of your soul because he listens and he cares. And he is more than capable of hearing all your needs because he is that big of a God.

The problem? We don't pray effectively. Scripture says to "cast our cares upon Him, for He cares for you" (1 Peter 5:7). See, we pray with our cares—but we don't cast them. If, by the end of your prayer, you are still holding onto burdens from when you started, you didn't cast your cares. You just vented them! God promises a peace to surpass your understanding when you pray (Philippians 4:6–7), but you cannot receive it if you've built a wall of worries to guard your heart. Cast your cares because prayer may not always change your situation—but it always changes you.

The purpose of prayer is not to get God to do our will. We don't pray to God, telling him our long list of wishes and wants. The purpose of prayer is to know God so we can do his will. Prayer is surrendering to God's will. Recall Jesus's prayer in the garden: "O Father, if it is possible, let this cup pass from Me; nevertheless, not as I will, but as You will" (Matthew 26:39). Facing the realities of the cross, Jesus surrendered his will to the Father through prayer, and it should be the same for us.

3. *Worship*

Worship is such a powerful tool because it takes the spotlight off you and puts it directly onto God. When you worship, you are laying aside all your fears, your doubts, and your worries to magnify the goodness of God. Praise forces you to make a faith decision that puts God's character over your circumstance. You are putting everything going on in your life aside to praise God based on his goodness and sovereignty alone.

What happens when we worship? Chains break. Prison walls collapse. Dead things come to life. Just like Paul and Silas in prison (Acts 16:22–26), when you worship, something happens inside of you. You are not the same. Because rather than letting your circumstance define you, you are allowing God to be everything you need in that particular situation. He is enough. King David said this in Psalm 145:1–3:

> I will extol you, my God, O King;
> And I will bless Your name forever and
> ever. Every day I will bless you, And I will
> praise Your name forever and ever. Great
> is the Lord, and greatly to be praised;
> And His greatness is unsearchable.

Notice the words David use. I will praise *your* name forever—because *you* are good. Worship aligns your heart with God's character.

Again, don't get this confused. These are some ways that can help you *build* your relationship with the Lord, not *earn* it. God never wanted you to feel obligated. His longing, desire has always been to know him in a deeper, more intimate way. And by the power of the Spirit, you can experience that today.

Grace Wins

Obedience is not an obligation but a *liberation.*

So what exactly is grace? We've talked about how God wants a relationship, not our religious efforts, and if love is the leading force, grace is the dominant factor. God's love is based on grace because it is *never* dependent on us. And if grace is what saves us, grace should bring freedom.

But—there's a problem. We abuse grace. We see grace as an excuse to sin and a way to justify what we want to do. Especially when we see our faith as a religion, we treat grace as a way to sin because, in the end, grace will just cover us up anyway. But as we've talked about, if you *truly* love Jesus, your number one priority will be to honor him with your life.

Key point: Grace isn't an excuse to sin. Grace is a *freedom* not to.

Grace isn't a means to justify the wrongs we've done. Grace is a freedom to say, "Because I am forgiven, I can live free. I can live away from the sin and shame because I am no longer held captive to what I've done." Just like the adulterous woman we talked about earlier, grace *freed* her. "Go and sin no more" (John 8:11).

Paul, one of the most prominent apostles from the New Testament, battled with this dilemma of grace. Throughout the book of Romans, we can see how he fought back and forth with this bondage and freedom of grace. And as we walk through it, I want you to make his words personal and read them as if they are applying directly to your life.

"What shall we say then? Shall we continue in sin that grace may abound? Certainly not! How shall we who died to sin live any longer in it?" (Romans 6:1–2).

Immediately, Paul makes it crystal clear—grace is not an excuse to sin. This is completely true. Just because we have grace doesn't give us the obligation to abuse it. Should we see grace as a way of bypassing our faults? Certainly not! Because if you really knew and loved God, you would not see grace as a free ticket toward evil. He also says in Romans 6:14, "For sin shall not have dominion over you, for you are not under law but under grace." You can live under the *freedom* of grace, not bondage to sin.

Romans 6 is Paul laying down the law. But—Paul is still human. And he battled with the same sins that we do. Look at what he says in Romans 7:

> For what I am doing, I do not understand. For what I will to do, that I do not practice; but what I hate, that I do. For the good that I will to do, I do not do; but the evil I will not to do, that I practice. But I see another law in my members, warring against the law of my mind, and bringing me into captivity to the law of sin which is in my members. (vv. 15, 19, 23)

Do you see? The same exact Paul who was adamant about not abusing grace was the same one who abused it. Paul did what he didn't want to do. And he says the power of sin still caught him sometimes.

Does this not sound like us? *God, I promise I won't ever do that again. That's my last time lying. That's my last time stealing. That's my last time lusting.* But after making promises we can't keep, we find ourselves in the same situation that we were in before—lost.

But Paul didn't stop there. Paul *knew* there was more—more love, more grace, more freedom.

There was more *Jesus*.

"O wretched man that I am! Who will deliver me from this body of death? I thank God—through Jesus Christ our Lord!" (Romans 7:24–25a).

"There is therefore now no condemnation to those who are in Christ Jesus, who do not walk according to the flesh, but according to the Spirit" (Romans 8:1).

Notice the shift of perspective and the journey Paul went on from Romans 6 to Romans 8. We see this trial and error of wanting to be like Christ yet falling short time and time again. So, how does Paul get transformed? He remembered the centerpiece of the gospel story—Jesus Christ. *Jesus* can save him from this life of sin and shame. Because if you *belong* to Christ Jesus, there is no more condemnation! That is extremely good news! Every sin you face, every battle you fight, every time you fall short, you can always count on one thing: Jesus brings no condemnation. And if you are in Christ, nothing in all of creation can separate you from the love of God (Romans 8:38–39).

In 1 Corinthians 15:51–53, Paul also talks about the resurrected bodies we will have when Jesus comes back. He also refers to this in Romans 8:23–25. It's important to understand that the bodies we live in now are *dead* to sin and will always be (Paul said this in Romans 7). However, when Jesus returns, we will be given *new* bodies that are sinless and glorified. Only then will we forever be freed from sin.

Romans 5:11 says, "And not only that, but we also rejoice in God through our Lord Jesus Christ, through whom we have now received the reconciliation." Because of the blood of Jesus, we have direct access to the throne and to God's heart. He is our replacement for the penalty of sin. And you find true freedom when you come to a middle ground of *striving* to die to sin with a realization that it will not be fully complete until Christ makes it complete, which is when he returns.

That is freedom. Knowing that yes, because you *love* the Lord, you do your very best not to sin. Even better, you chase after his heart and leave sin in the dust. You understand there is a *better* life Jesus is inviting you to. But you also realize that because we have not received our heavenly bodies, we will always have trouble overcoming sin. Paul demonstrates here the freedom and depth of grace, of how, even in our sin, his love outweighs the fault. Because God doesn't look at our sins—he looks at Jesus's scars. And he loves us way farther than the east is from the west and has removed *every* transgression from us (Psalm 103:12).

Romans 5:20 tells us that "where sin abounded, grace abounded much more." Wherever there is sin, there is *more* grace. Wherever there is hurt, there is *more* grace. Wherever there is shame, there is *more* of God's grace! His grace always outweighs the sin, no matter where we are or what we've done.

It all goes back to the same point we've highlighted all along. If we look at faith in Jesus as a *relationship,* our life will reflect it. We will do our very best to keep his commandments and honor him with our life. However, we're still human and we still sin. But his love and his grace are stronger than the worst desires inside us. His mercy is enough. And when you come to understand this freedom of grace that he offers, you finally start to see him in a deeper, intimate way.

Why does this matter? Because if you truly value your relationship with Jesus, you will have a longing, desire to obey him. This is *good* news and a freeing liberation that reminds us of the goodness of God. Grace isn't an excuse to sin. Grace is a freedom not to sin. And because of grace, I can live a new life away from sin and run toward Christ.

I'm not concerned with obeying law. I'm focused on knowing Jesus.

Transformation > Modification

Okay, I'm starting to get it. God wants me to know him in an intimate way, and that comes from seeking him, not trying to impress him. He wants a relationship with me. But what about my behavior? What does he think about that? Sure, I follow him and say I know him, but I haven't seen a real behavior shift. Now what?

If you're anything like me, you've had this thought in your head before: *Why can't I change? I mean, I love God and love Jesus. I've accepted him as Lord. I know that his grace covers my sins, but still—I see no change in the way I live. Will I* LOSE *this grace he is giving me? Does he think any less of me?*

This is one of the most important sections in understanding the entire book. Why? Because it answers the questions about behavior and transformation. Remember, if God wants our heart, he wants a genuine longing to seek and know him. And with that comes change.

Religion says, you have to *go* to God with good works. You must already be perfected and live a good life before you ever try to get right with him. The problem? We can't do that. It is incredibly hard for us, if not impossible, to live exactly the way God wants us to. These are two big points about how religion actually lowers our chances at seeing a behavior modification:

1. When focusing on the poison of religion, you forget the power of grace.
2. Religion is our attempt to *earn* God's favor by following all the rules.

This is the problem with religion. We focus way too much on how we *should* come to Jesus, instead of actually just *coming to Jesus*. We put more effort into being good enough, rather than accepting the fact that he wants us to come as we are. And when we treat our faith as religion, we think when we don't meet the bar of morality, we might as well stop there and quit altogether.

We try way too hard to perform, instead of trusting his Spirit to transform.

First John 2:6 says, "He who says he abides in Him ought himself also to walk just as He walked." Obviously, there's more to this whole relationship thing than just accepting grace. Because truth be told, a real sign of a genuine repentant heart will be a life transformation. But how? That's what we're going to look at now. Remember our key word for this book—*abide*. First John 2 tells us right here that if we abide in him, we should also walk as he walked.

Here's the catch: the more we seek him, the more he will transform us. *That's* how transformation happens! We don't just, one day, change in our own power. Rather, over time, the more we come to him and the more we grow to know him, the more *he* changes us.

It's not a behavior modification. It's a spiritual transformation.

"I say then: Walk in the Spirit, and you shall not fulfill the lust of the flesh. But if you are led by the Spirit, you are not under the law" (Galatians 5:16, 18).

Paul tells us right here how we can experience transformation: walk by the Spirit. The more we walk *by* him and experience his goodness, the more we open our hearts up to allow him to change us. We don't go to him perfect; rather, the more we *seek* him, the more he transforms us. Take the fruits of the Spirit for example. Galatians 5:22–23 tells us, "But the fruit of the Spirit is love, joy, peace, long-suffering, goodness, faithfulness, gentleness, self-control." All these attributes are not things you *have* to do in order to come to Jesus. These are fruits that are a *by-product* of walking by the Spirit! Paul is saying here that the more you walk by him, the more you will see this spiritual harvest bear fruit. It's the same with spiritual disciplines; the more you walk and know him intimately, the more you will *want* to honor your disciplines. And remember, it's not *your* power. You aren't the harvester here of these spiritual seeds.

It's the same with the works of the flesh. Just like spiritual fruit is a by-product of walking by the Spirit, works of the flesh can be identified the more you *don't* know Jesus. Galatians 5:19–21 lists them as "adultery, fornication, uncleanness, lewdness, idolatry, sorcery, hatred, contentions, jealousies, outbursts of wrath, selfish ambitions, etc." This isn't a list to tell you how bad of a person you are. These are things that you *will* see in your life as a by-product if you don't know Jesus well. And this goes with everything the Bible talks about. Loving others, forgiving, serving, living pure—the fruits of the Spirit and works of the flesh are not *rules* you have to follow. They are simply *by-products* of knowing or not knowing Jesus in a super intimate way.

It's a relationship, not a religion.

The more you try to work your way to being a good person, the less you will experience the Spirit transform you. It's not in *your* power. You will never be able to go to Jesus, already thinking you're perfect, and experience his love and goodness in a radical way. However, if you go to him broken and in need of healing and saving, over time, the more you seek him and grow to know him, he will change you. It's a cause and effect of *knowing* him, not trying to impress him.

But—be careful. The more you walk and grow with Jesus in this intimate way, the more spiritual opposition you will feel. The more you seek Jesus, the more the devil will try to pull you away. Remember the verse we referred to at the beginning of this book: "The thief does not come except to steal, kill, and destroy. I have come that they may have life, and that they have it more abundantly" (John 10:10). Don't get discouraged by spiritual opposition. Because the more you start to feel opposition, the more you will know you're fighting a good fight.

Now, look at the word Paul used in Galatians 5:16—*walk*. What he didn't say was *run* by the Spirit. Like all relationships, change takes time. It takes time, seeking Jesus and knowing his heart to experience transformation, so don't feel discouraged when you don't feel anything right away. Remember, your job isn't to harvest the fruit. Your job is to plant the seeds. And Galatians 6:8 tells us, "For he who sows to the Spirit will of the Spirit reap everlasting life." Stop trying so hard to be perfect. Because if you focus first on just knowing and growing in Jesus, he will do the change for you. John 14:26 says,

"But the Helper, the Holy Spirit, whom the Father will send in My name, he will teach you all things, and bring to you remembrance all things I said to you." You don't have to come to him perfect. You just have to come as you are.

Because *he* is the one who does the transforming in your life. The more you stop trying to do the work yourself, the more you'll start trusting him to do the work in you.

Religion says, "Try harder," but relationship says, "Trust more."

"Why? Because they did not seek it by faith, but as it were, by the works of the law. For they stumbled at that stumbling stone" (Romans 9:32).

Fear of God

When I was a kid, I can distinctly remember one Sunday morning at church where I left the building scared. And when I say scared, I mean I was genuinely afraid. Afraid of what, you might ask? Well, this is what the pastor said: "*It is good for your soul when you grow to fear the Lord.*"

Fear the Lord? Uh…whatever you say. I guess I'll be afraid of God. He is kind of big and scary anyway. I mean, I can't even see him! And over time, after misusing this term, I found myself as a young child genuinely being afraid of God. I would pray to him every night. "God, *please* don't send me to hell! Please don't send me to hell!" I took this term of *fear of the Lord* (that is actually found in Scripture) way out of context.

Truth be told, we all *should* ought to fear the Lord. The problem is, we don't know what that means. But if you look at Scripture and really see the power of fearing the Lord and what it means, it will change your faith drastically. Because your original perspective of God changes from convicting judge to loving Father.

"The fear of the Lord is the beginning of knowledge, but fools despise wisdom and instruction" (Proverbs 1:7).

"The fear of the Lord leads to life, and he who has it will abide in satisfaction; he will not be visited with evil" (Proverbs 19:23).

Obviously, from what Scripture says, fearing the Lord is good. It has knowledge, it leads to life, it satisfies, and it must be something in our Christian walk. So what does it mean? Very simply put, fear of the Lord is a combination of a *love* for God and a *respect* for God.

Fear of the Lord is not God telling you to be afraid of him. Fear of the Lord is a combination of love and respect for him. *I love you, Lord. Your undeserving grace for me brings me incredible joy, and I am so grateful for it. I love you as my Father. But at the same time, I also recognize you are the creator of the universe. And I respect you for your sovereignty, your divinity, and your power.*

Fear of the Lord is a result of respecting him enough for controlling the entire universe yet loving him enough because he cares about you.

The word for *fear* used in Proverbs 1:7 in Hebrew is *yirah*, which means "extreme reverence and respect." It all goes back to the same point we've highlighted all along: If you grow to love God in an intimate way, you will have a longing, desire to keep his commandments. John 14:23 says, "If anyone loves me, he will keep My word; and my Father loves him, and we will come to him and make Our home with him." This cause and effect is the intent of the heart that God has longed for all along. If we *really* love God for who he is, we will do our very best to keep his word. Our number one priority in everything we do will be to honor him with our choices, our decisions, and, ultimately, our lives. Also, note what Jesus says at the end of the verse, "We will come to him and make Our home with him." The more we *abide* in him, wanting to relationally love and honor him with our lives, the more we will open our hearts up to welcome his presence.

That's what fear of the Lord is. Fear of the Lord is not "because I am scared of God, I will follow all of his rules." Fear of the Lord is "because I *love* and *respect* God, I *want* to honor him with my life." Will I be perfect? Most likely not. But my top priority through all my days is to follow his will and his way—because he is worthy of it.

Why is this so important to have? Because if we really want to see a deep, intimate relationship built with Jesus in our lives, it starts with *submission*. The moment we surrender is the moment we put aside *our* wants and wills and upgrade them with his. The entire Christian life is surrender in that, every day, you are denying yourself and following him (Matthew 16:24). So when you fear God, you are obeying *not* because you're afraid of any repercussions but because you love God enough and *want* obedience. Joseph, an Old Testament leader, said this while being sexually tempted by Potiphar's wife: "How then can I do this great wickedness, and sin against God?" (Genesis 39:9). See the perspective of where Joseph was coming from? Joseph wasn't thinking that getting with this chick was against the rules. His greatest concern was not a religious boundary. Joseph was genuinely against the thought of turning against such a God he loved. And because he loved and respected God so much, he did not give in to sin.

This is where we should be. You want to see transformation in your life? It starts with two predetermined choices to love and respect the Lord. Scripture promises that the fear of the Lord is the beginning of knowledge and leads to life. And if we approach things with this perspective, we always will prioritize obedience.

Again, not because we *have* to but because we *want* to. He's good enough to deserve it.

Redeemed

To close out this chapter, I want to look at a beautiful story that captures the point we've highlighted so distinctly. As we know, God prioritizes a genuine relationship with us over a half-hearted attempt at following him based on works. And the good news is, no matter how far you run or how lost you think you are, you are never too far to outrun his love. He wants you to come as you are, broken and in need of healing, so he can mend you back together into the person you were created to be. And a great story to capture this involves a very unlikely character: Peter.

We have all heard of Peter. There are plenty of good stories about Peter—but there are also plenty of bad ones. Funny ones, even. But out of everything Peter did, probably the most infamous thing we all know of is when he denied Jesus three times. And because of this great sin, Peter felt an enormous wave of guilt and shame, pulling him away from God. And as we walk through this story, put yourself in Peter's shoes. Wherever you are in your walk, see how loving the Father's arms are and how open they are for reconciliation.

A little backstory may help. Peter's name wasn't actually Peter; it was Simon. But Jesus changed his name to Peter (which means "the rock"). Peter was that one friend you have that always causes you to make funny faces at them. He would act first then think second, always leaving room for either humiliation or regret. And because Peter was so quick to act without thinking, he often found himself in situations he truly didn't want to be in that would cost him everything.

At the Last Supper, hours before Jesus went into the Garden of Gethsemane, it was revealed that someone would eventually betray Jesus (Luke 22:21–22, Judas of Iscariot betrayed him). Obviously, Jesus already knew who it would be, but the other disciples, sitting around him, didn't. So Peter, without hesitation, immediately boasted about how faithful and obedient he was to Jesus all along. He would *never* betray Jesus like that. And after claiming it was basically impossible that he would do such a thing, Jesus told Peter that "before the rooster crows today, you will deny Me three times that you know Me" (Luke 22:34).

Right about now, sitting at the table, Peter's probably feeling a mixture of extreme pride and extreme panic. *I would never do such a thing. I'm such a good disciple! But what if I do? I just don't know. Who knows. Hey, John, pass me the bread, will ya?* And even after Peter strongly conveyed he would stay faithful, Jesus even tells Peter Satan has asked to "sift him like wheat" (Luke 22:31). Jesus was allowing Peter to go through something because he knew the redemption he could give Peter on the other side. And right before they went out to the garden, Jesus finished with, "But I have prayed for you, that your faith should not fail; and when you have returned to Me, strengthen your brethren" (Luke 22:32).

The meal finished. They all went to the garden. Judas betrayed Jesus. And Peter even cut off one of the guard's ears in defense that they wouldn't capture him (Luke 22:50). Peter was so caught up in all the *acts* of faithfulness that he totally forgot the real relationship with Jesus. Because after Jesus was led into the courtyard to be beaten, mocked, and scorned, Peter followed from a distance. And now, it was crunch time.

As Peter stood from afar, watching Jesus bear the punishment, three separate times, people accused him of being a disciple. So what did Peter do? He denied all three accusations. And as soon as the third denial happened, the rooster crowed, and Peter was torn. Scripture even says he was extremely remorseful and wept bitterly (Luke 22:62).

Peter was lost. Just like we get today, after trying to meet the bar with so many good works and signs of obedience, he fell apart. Sin gave way, and Peter was emotionally unstable. Peter was so far away from simply true intimacy and devotion to Christ that his good works pulled him *away* from Christ. But the story went on. Jesus went to the cross (even for Peter's sins); three days later, he rose again, and a couple of days after that, he had an encounter in John 21 with Peter.

The story takes place with Jesus walking up to the sea where Peter and some other disciples were out fishing. (Notice how Jesus *still* sought after Peter, even amidst his own sins). Now, remember— Peter was *originally* a fisherman. Days after his wave of guilt, he returned to his old job and his old way of living. He was ashamed. He didn't believe a shameful fisherman could carry the calling Jesus had originally placed on his life. He went back to comfort—an old place he knew because he was too afraid to get back up and go to God in need of healing.

Sounds like us? We do the same thing today. After all our efforts of trying to please God, the moment we fall off, we run away in shame. We think what we did causes him to look at us differently, and with our scars in hand, we hide them and put them away for safekeeping. Just like Peter, we go to an old place we know good and well, hardly believing we could be restored and loved again. But that isn't the end to this story. Jesus stood on shore, and after hearing they caught *zero* fish (John 21:4–5), he told them to place the net on a different side of the boat.

Jesus basically said this: *"How's that way working for you? How are your old ways turning out? Not so good. You returned to a comfortable place. Any progress? Not really. Still going back to those old ways? It's okay. Try it this way instead."*

Why was it different when Jesus told them to go somewhere else? Because it was an opportunity for the disciples (mostly Peter) to follow Jesus's voice—a restoration, a renewal, a restart. This was their chance to start over and find redemption.

Not surprisingly, they ended up catching 153 fish (v. 11) and brought them onto shore. And after Jesus offered to have breakfast with them, he said some key words to Peter that conclude the theme from this story. At that very moment, Jesus had every right to shame Peter. *"You're a hypocrite. You're worthless. Good for nothing. All you do is talk the talk."* But instead, he invited Peter to eat (John 21:12). Peter was not only welcomed but encouraged to return.

This is the most important part. Jesus asks Peter three times if he loved him, and after Peter said yes, Jesus said, "Then feed My lambs" (v. 15).

Basically, Jesus said this: *"Peter, if you love me, get back on the horse and do my work. Your calling hasn't gone away, and my purposes for your life haven't changed. So go. I'm with you. I'm for you. And because you came to me broken, I'm ready to heal and restore you to use you in a big way."*

Peter, crawling out of shame, went on to save three thousand people and bring them to Christ (story told in Acts 2). Because he recognized Jesus's grace was bigger than his guilt, he understood that Jesus never wanted perfection—he just wanted his heart.

And it's the same for you. Peter was drowning in despair with no way out. After all the good works he tried to do, he still ended up in the same pit of shame he started in. But after coming to Jesus as he was, isolated and in need of restoration, Jesus did a work in him that not only changed his life but three thousand others as well.

This is what he has wanted all along—just simply for you to *come.* Just like Peter, after finally realizing he wasn't too far from Jesus, he embraced the fact that God prioritized real intimacy over some behavior show. And once Peter *did* find the intimacy he wanted, only then was God able to do something through him that made a difference. See, Peter wasn't perfect. He didn't go to Jesus already spotless and clean. But once he did, Jesus changed his heart inside out and made him into all he was created to be.

And so can you. You were created for so much more. And the good news is, it doesn't take a miracle. All you have to do is come to Jesus.

CHAPTER 3

Trials Form Testimonies

Purpose in the Pain

As a young kid, whenever the holidays rolled around, my family and I would always take a trip down to Georgia. We would stay at my grandparents' house for a couple days and spend time with the ones we loved. I always enjoyed being around my grandparents, but there was a certain trip we had one year where something happened that I would never forget.

My grandfather used to be a big hunter. Back when he was consistently out in the field, he would go on serious hunting trips to track down animals who were messing up farmers' crops and materials. And because he was so intrigued in hunting, he was also into other weapons that you could shoot with. So one holiday, out of tree branches and string, he made bow and arrows for me and my younger brother.

Pretty cool, right? I would say so. As soon as I got my bow and arrow, I ran outside and started shooting it around. Now because the weapon was made from tree branches and string, the arrow itself was a stick with a sharp point at the end. So when I was shooting it, I always had to be careful where I was shooting at so nobody could get injured in any way. My grandfather probably told me a thousand times not to shoot it at someone's direction because he didn't want anyone getting hurt. He trusted me to handle something in the proper way for everyone to benefit from it.

Finally, after a good amount of time shooting and running after my arrow, my grandpa told me it was time to go inside and eat. He wanted me to give him the bow and arrow so I wouldn't break or lose it. He said, "Come bring it to me, Ryan." But the problem was, I *really* wanted to shoot the arrow one last time. I was having a blast! So I tried to angle the bow exactly right to where, if I shot the arrow, it would land about ten feet short of him and slide the rest of the way for him to pick up.

After quickly thinking about how smart this decision was (not really), I raised my bow, pulled back the arrow, aimed right at my grandfather, and shot. I watched as the arrow slid up to his feet, thinking I was a genius for calculating such a feat. But when I saw his face and looked in his eyes, I could tell he wasn't very happy with me.

Very calmly, he shouted out to me, "Bring that bow here."

So I walked up to him, trying to figure out what he was going to do, and gave him my bow. And to my disappointment, I watched as he picked up the arrow, grabbed the bow, and broke both over his knee. My toy was destroyed. I no longer had a bow and arrow and went running inside very ashamed of what I had done.

At that moment, as a young kid, I was heartbroken. I couldn't imagine why my grandpa would do such a thing. Was he mad at me? Did I deserve it? Was this punishment? But today, looking back on the story, I see how my grandpa wasn't punishing me for what I had done but teaching me something for other scenarios I would have in life. Sure, I no longer had a bow and arrow, but that day, I learned a valuable lesson about listening to someone when they tell me something out of my best interest. That day, I learned something I would carry the rest of my life.

So far, we have talked a lot about how God wants a deep and intimate relationship with his children. Not only do we not deserve his love but the fact that he made a way for us through Jesus Christ should draw us closer to the throne. But reality is, just because you may *know* Jesus well doesn't mean your life will suddenly become a lot easier. We still live in a broken world, and we still go through trials and tribulations. And the problem is, so many people think that because they go through hard times, God doesn't love them and God doesn't care. Or worse, God *really isn't that good.*

The fact of the matter is, just because you have Jesus in your corner doesn't mean you won't face storms. Jesus even said it himself in John 16:33, "These things I have spoken to you, that in Me you may have peace. In the world you will have tribulation; but be of good cheer, I have overcome the world." The promise here is not that Jesus will eliminate all of life's troubles when you start to know him. The promise is that he can be your *peace* in the middle of it because he has already overcome.

When it comes to trials we face in life, we must change our perspective from pain to purpose. Because if we *really* want to build faith in the Lord, it comes from intimately getting to know him when things get rough. Second Corinthians 5:7 says, "Walk by faith and not by sight." Hebrews 11:6 also says that it is "*impossible* to please God without faith" (italicization mine). Obviously, growing and knowing the Lord in an intimate way comes from believing he is good, even when we can't see it.

When my grandfather broke my bow, I thought that the *lesson* he was teaching me was a *punishment* he was giving me. But that's simply not the case. Just like my grandpa, sometimes, God allows things in our lives to *force* us to let go of our own strength and rely on him completely. God doesn't want to punish you; hard times aren't given just because he wants you to go through them. Rather, God is trying to *teach* you something and *draw* you closer to him in the middle of it. I wasn't *ready* to receive such a blessing yet, so in preparation, something happened *to* me that would radically do a change *in* me.

Maybe, because we aren't fully ready yet, God doesn't change our situations because he is more concerned about changing us first.

Think about how I felt when the bow and arrow broke—*snap!* In that moment, I believed that my *grandfather* wasn't good to me because of something else that happened in my life. Instead of trusting the purpose behind a scenario, I immediately blamed the one who had control of the scenario anyway. We do the same with God.

We think just because something bad happens in our lives that God doesn't care or God doesn't want our best. But in the same way, I came out better on the other side. God does a work in us *through* the pain that forms who we will soon become.

It's not just a trial. It's a testimony.

Over the next chapter, we are going to dive deep into finding purpose in pain and how going through trials actually brings us closer to Christ. Let me warn you—not everything is going to be your typical feel-good message. But if you *really* want to get closer to Jesus, you have to understand that it takes extreme faith to rely on him when things get tough. And when you are going through hard times, you bet it takes some crazy faith.

Faith under Trials

What's the purpose of going through trials? What good can come out of tough times? Sometimes, when our faith gets shaken, we begin to wonder if there's even a purpose in the pain. As we've talked about all along, God desires a deep, intimate relationship with you and me. And the truth is, if we are ever going to experience that, it's going to take something more, not just an easy road to pass by but a shadow of death to walk *through*. Just like King David said in Psalm 23, "I will fear no evil, for You are with me; Your rod and Your staff, they comfort me" (v. 4).

The faith statement here from David is *not* "because you are with me, I will have an easy life." The faith statement is "even if I walk through the valley, you still comfort me." Tough times are inevitable, but they serve a purpose when you see them as an opportunity to lean more into God and his faithfulness to sustain.

James 1:2–4 says:

> My brethren, count it all joy when you fall into various trials, knowing that the testing of your faith produces patience. But let patience have its perfect work, that you may be perfect and complete, lacking nothing.

James here says to count it as *joy* when you go through hard times. Why? Because in the middle of the pain, your faith is experiencing a radical transformation it wouldn't have otherwise experienced. If we look at pain from a perspective of purpose, you'll see that in the middle of uncertainty, you are growing to trust and lean on God more and more. The situation is out of your control—so you give it up to the one who is.

For many of us today, our faith can be summed up into two words: *What if?* This kind of faith is based on our circumstances and position of responses. When we possess a what-if kind of faith, we are hoping that every bad outcome we think of doesn't happen. Our faith in God *begs* him to step in and do something so we don't have to experience a tough time. *God, please don't let me go through this.* The only problem is, it leaves us stranded and lacking any source of deep, relational trust.

Rather, our faith should sound like this: "*Even if.*" An even-if kind of faith is no longer based on *our* circumstances but *God's* character. God's goodness isn't just a mood, it's an attribute. He isn't good sometimes, when he feels like it; he is the literal definition of goodness itself! When your faith is based on who God is, no matter what happens, you can maintain course because you aren't trusting in a peaceful outcome but a peaceful Savior. Remember, you *will* walk through the valley of the shadow of death. But fear not because, although you are indeed walking, you aren't walking alone.

Yes, we serve a God that can move mountains. Yes, we serve a God who can part the waters. And should we believe he can? Absolutely. Believing that God can make a way through anything is the type of faith he desires. But connecting our faith to his character creates such a deeper level of trust. Because then, you are no longer believing he is good for what he does but, rather, believing he is good for *who he is.*

Now, step back for a minute. How does this deepen our relationship with Jesus? If you *really* want to know Jesus intimately, you have to base your trust on his love. Jesus never changes; Scripture says he is the same yesterday, today, and forever (Hebrews 13:8). So if you *truly* know him in an intimate way, you are faithfully standing on the promise that no matter what I go through, he is faithful. No matter how I feel, he is still working. No matter what I experience, he can still turn me around. And even if it doesn't go my way, I *know* that he is still good.

Good, not just because of what he does but for who he is.

Remember, hardships aren't just for your personal growth either. Hardships *glorify* God and his goodness, even amid tribulation. His glory is magnified and reflected through each mountain he moves. Will it be hard? Most likely, yes. Going through discipline isn't easy but always promises a deeper reward in the end. Think back to how my grandpa broke my bow and arrow. Did he know it would hurt me on the inside? Probably. But he also knew I would (1) learn from it and (2) love and respect him more after it was all said and done. It's the same way with God. Although there may be pain, we can trust in the promise that there is always a purpose. It's always good for us in the end.

The problem that we so often face is that we mistakenly connect peace to circumstance. We think that because our problems are absent, our peace is present. But that's not the promise in Scripture. Peace isn't the absence of storms—peace is a comfort *through* the storm. Isaiah 26:3–4 says, "You will keep him in perfect peace, whose mind is stayed on You, because he trusts in You. Trust in the Lord forever, for in Yah, the Lord, is everlasting strength."

Maybe you haven't *experienced* peace because you don't *know* the prince of peace.

Can I challenge you? Base God's goodness on who he is, not just what he does. Does God do good things for us? Heck, yeah, he does. But when you base his goodness on his character and *who* he is, your perception of him never changes. *My God is good, period. He is faithful. He is full of love. He is gracious, kind, and merciful to me. And over anything else I face, him sending Jesus was my greatest gift. Even if I face tough times, I know he has already saved me eternally—so I will rejoice.* We change. Our circumstances change. But he never does. And when you have the faith to endure trials, knowing he is doing something to your heart, only then will you reap the harvest of trusting him through every season and every storm.

Light in the Dark

When life is going well, it's easy to love God. It's easy to be on good terms with God when everything's going your way and there aren't any problems. But what happens when life changes? How do you stand firm in faith when you face a mountain? Sure, we know and love Jesus. But sometimes, we fall into a dangerous place where—if our life isn't good, we conclude *he* is not good either.

Everyone enjoys God when we're on a mountaintop. But it's only through the valley where we experience him in a deep, intimate way.

It's easy praising God when life is good, but it takes faith to praise him when things get tough. And over this next section, we are going to look at an Old Testament prophet who had his faith severely tested when he went through a storm: Habakkuk. Throughout the Old Testament, God utilized prophets to speak to the people on his behalf. He would use these chosen prophets to explain to the Israelites his will for them. But Habakkuk was different; unlike the other prophets, Habakkuk spoke to *God* on behalf of the *people*. Instead of God using Habakkuk to move the hearts of the people, Habakkuk spoke for the people to move the heart of God!

Habakkuk's name in Hebrew literally translates to *wrestle and embrace*. This is so cool to me because, as we will see in Scripture, Habakkuk had to *wrestle and embrace* in his faith with the Lord. During the time Habakkuk was written, the people of Israel were in severe bondage and oppression. God's chosen people had turned against him, and God allowed them to be persecuted and oppressed because of their sin. But after turning from their evil ways and repenting to God, they hoped for saving and redemption in their land. The only problem is—that hadn't happened yet.

> O Lord, how long shall I cry, and You will
> not hear? Even cry out to You, "Violence!" and
> You will not save. Why do You show me iniquity,
> and cause me to see trouble? For plundering and

violence are before me; there is strife, and contention arises. (Habakkuk 1:2–3)

God, where are you? Are you still good? All I do is cry for help, but you don't listen. I want to trust you so bad, but it is very hard when life gets tough. I'm sure we can relate. When our faith gets shaken, we find it so easy to step away from God and forget he is good. We connect what we *see* to how we *view* God—the total opposite of walking by faith. And reality is, if life was *always* easy, it wouldn't take any faith to begin with.

God responds to Habakkuk: "Look among the nations and watch—be utterly astounded! For I will work a work in your days which you would not believe, though it were told you" (Habakkuk 1:5). Yes! Finally, some good news. God answered my prayer, *and* he's going to tell me what's going to happen. And better yet, it's a surprise! Can't wait.

But it wasn't good news.

"For indeed I am raising up the Chaldeans, a bitter and hasty nation which marches through the breadth of the earth, to possess dwelling places *that are* not theirs" (Habakkuk 1:6).

Wait a second. Time-out. Habakkuk is pleading with God to help him and the people find freedom. But instead of promising deliverance, God promises to raise up the Babylonians! These people were the fiercest conquerors of the day and would eventually exile the Israelites for seventy years. The moment Habakkuk hoped that God would come in and save the day, he tells him things are about to get a lot worse.

Listen to Habakkuk wrestle and embrace with God:

Are You not from everlasting, O Lord my God, my Holy One? We shall not die. O Lord, You have appointed them for judgment; O Rock, You have marked them for correction. You are of purer eyes than to behold evil, and cannot look on wickedness. Why do You look on those who deal treacherously, and hold Your tongue when the wicked devours A person more righteous than he? (Habakkuk 1:12–13)

God, you are holy, but is this really what you had in mind? Surely, you can't do this. Notice how Habakkuk didn't just brush off his circumstance to the side. He emotionally confronted God with big faith questions and poured out what was on his heart.

When we go through tough times, it's easy for us to ball up in a corner and stay away from God. But as Habakkuk proves here, God is *big* enough to take your worries. Cry out to him. Ask him questions. Because it takes *faith* to stay in the mix when things are uncertain.

It takes faith to wrestle and embrace.

Notice that Habakkuk didn't just walk away. He *entered* the valley yet did not climb out of it from the same side. Because everyone enjoys God on the mountaintops, but you intimately get to know him through the valleys. You always feel good about God when life is good. But you get to really know who he is when life gets tough.

Can you feel his pain? His doubts? His sense of injustice? He goes on to remind God that God was the one who chose the people who are now punishing the innocent. And with an almost sarcastic tone, he says "You can't even look at evil, but you are allowing it." Like many of us, Habakkuk can't figure out why God doesn't do what he thinks God should do.

Keep in mind that Habakkuk is a man who loves God! This is a Bible story, not an angry post from someone on Instagram. Habakkuk didn't hold back, and neither should you. God can handle any question, cry, or shouts of anger we dare to ask him. He doesn't get angry when we ask. He understands. Even when we are pouring out our deepest burdens, he wants us to draw closer to himself. We have his permission to speak freely.

So, what happens to Habakkuk? He wrestles with his faith, and he embraces his reality. The Babylonians are coming, but that doesn't automatically mean that God isn't good. He says in chapter 2, "But the Lord is in His holy temple, let all the earth be silent before Him" (v. 20). After everything he's gone through and all the emotions he's experienced, Habakkuk says three incredibly powerful words: "*But the Lord.*" But the Lord! Sure, I'm going through a tough time—but the Lord. Sure, I can't see a way out—but the Lord. Sure, my future seems uncertain and I can feel my faith wavering—but the Lord. These three powerful words completely disregard what's going on in his life and put the spotlight straight onto God and his goodness. God even told Habakkuk in chapter 2 that "the righteous shall live by faith" (v. 4). Habakkuk remembered the reality: he's still on the throne. And when we feel like all hope seems lost in our own lives, we should do the same.

When we go through difficult times, the best way to deepen our faith is to remind ourselves of God's goodness. Even when we can't necessarily see it in the present moment, it's important to remember he is still faithful and he is still good. Habakkuk prays, "O Lord, I have heard Your speech and was afraid; O Lord, revive Your work in the midst of the years! In the midst of the years make it known; in wrath remember mercy" (Habakkuk 3:2). There's a respectful, appreciative tone to the way he begins here. It's almost as if he was saying, "Well, if I'm being honest God, I've experienced times before where your presence seemed more real than now. You were doing big things then, and I know that's the kind of God you are. But please do those same kinds of things again for us now. Do again what you've done before." In fact, the Hebrew word that's translated *repeat* here is *cha-yah*, which simply means "to restore, revive, and renew." Remind yourself who God is. Know what he has done before and know what he can do again. You must revive your heart and renew your mind with the truth of God—who he is and what he does. He is for you, not against you. And he is working all things for your good.

And even in the middle of speculation, that's where faith comes in. It's always easy to worship God when you're on a mountaintop. But when you're in the valley, that's where your belief in him is proven and tested beyond measure. It's comfortable praising God for blessings. But thanking God for what he hasn't done takes faith. And that's where Habakkuk gets to as he closes out his prayer:

> Though the fig tree may not blossom, nor fruit be on the vines; though the labor of the olive may fail, and the fields yield no food; though the flock may be cut off from the fold, and there be no herd in the stalls—Yet I will rejoice in the Lord, I will joy in the God of my salvation. The Lord God is my strength; He will make my feet like deer's feet, and He will make me walk on my high hills. (Habakkuk 3:17–19)

Even if I don't see it,
Even when I don't feel it,
Even if it doesn't go my way,
Even if it hasn't happened yet,
Even if my prayer hasn't been answered,
Even if everyone else is against me,
Even if the outcome isn't in my favor,
Even though the trees don't blossom,
I will rejoice in the Lord.
Even when the crops fail, I will rejoice in the Lord.

God, even when I don't see it, you're working! What a huge faith statement from Habakkuk here. Because it doesn't matter what I go through—I am choosing to be joyful in the God of my salvation. This even-if faith Habakkuk reflects here is where we ought to be. Because it doesn't matter what I go through—I believe my God can be good, even if my life is not.

Habakkuk wasn't imprisoned, but he demonstrated a kind of faith we must have when we face terrible circumstances. After everything he experienced and went through, he was able to remember what God has done, accept what God was doing, and trust what God was soon to do. Habakkuk realized that, no matter what he went through, he was surrounded by the living Lord of hosts. And in the end, his faith was sharpened and strengthened because of a certain trial God walked him through in his life.

Remember: It's *easy* to praise God when life is good. But if we are seeking a deep, intimate, abiding relationship with Jesus, it's going to take faith! When things get tough and we kick in our even-if faith, we experience a trust that would never have been evident otherwise. Because you will *never* love God completely just for what he gives but for who he is. It all goes back to how he is molding you and your faith into everything he is preparing you to be.

Wait on the Lord. Because in due time, he will strengthen your weary soul (Isaiah 40:31).

Not a Hostage

Some of you, in a season of uncertainty, may feel like you were placed there with no purpose or no provision. It wasn't God's plan all along; you were randomly inserted into a tough time, and there is no way out. But the truth is, God works *all* things for our good (Romans 8:28). And if we really want to increase our intimacy with Jesus, we must understand how there is always a purpose in the pain. We are never alone.

One of my favorite perspectives out of all the New Testament comes from Paul, a converted apostle of Jesus. After being thrown into prison for preaching about Christ, Paul wrote multiple books of the Bible from a jail cell. How crazy is that? And we are going to see here in Philippians how Paul didn't let his circumstance dictate his purpose; rather, Paul found purpose, no matter what circumstance he was in.

To give context, Philippians was written obviously from a position of arrest but also while being chained to a prison guard. Every eight hours, a new guard would come watch over Paul as he wrote this letter to the church of Philippi. This was what he said:

> But I want you to know, brethren, that
> the things which happened to me have actually
> turned out for the furtherance of the gospel, so

> that it has become evident to the whole palace
> guard, and to all the rest, that my chains are in
> Christ; and most of the brethren in the Lord,
> having become confident by my chains, are
> much more bold to speak the word without fear.
> (Philippians 1:12–14)

I hope that you feel the power in Paul's words here. As Paul was *chained* and *imprisoned,* he says that *everything* had a purpose! Not only was he still alive but Paul actually *used* his chains to bring the prison guards to Christ! In the middle of complete uncertainty, Paul took what seemed like a bad situation and turned it into an opportunity to spread the good news of the gospel.

Paul was *not* a hostage.

Paul could have so easily begin to doubt. *God doesn't want me to serve here. My ideas are useless. I'm screwed. I can't even go preach for crying out loud because I'm stuck here in prison.* But he didn't. Instead, he used his situation and turned it into a way of spreading the gospel. Scripture says that "everyone knew he was in chains for Christ" (v. 13), and most of the believers in prison had now grown to speak boldly about the goodness of God.

This is what Paul understood: he was *placed* in that jail on purpose. He was not a hostage. He was not a victim of random events and uncertain circumstances where he just happened to fall out of God's hands and lose his way. Remember, this is the same Paul who, in the same book, wrote:

> Rejoice in the Lord always. Again I will say,
> rejoice! Let your gentleness be known to all men.
> The Lord is at hand. Be anxious for nothing, but
> in everything by prayer and supplication, with
> thanksgiving, let your requests be made known
> to God; and the peace of God, which surpasses
> all understanding, will guard your hearts and
> minds through Christ Jesus. (Philippians 4:4–7)

The Paul who was chained in prison was the same Paul who said, "Be anxious for nothing." How can it be? Because no matter the circumstance, Paul trusted and believed that God knew what he was doing and was using it for the greater good.

Paul wasn't a captive to his circumstances or fears. That's a lot to be writing from a prison cell, possibly awaiting your death penalty. But Paul wrote it anyway. He passionately continued to fight the good fight of faith and spread the gospel. He didn't let his *situation* dictate his *mission*. He didn't allow his present emotions to override his *eternal goal*. He was alive for one reason—he wanted to preach the gospel.

Paul wasn't a hostage. And neither are you.

You are not a hostage. The circumstances you're in don't define who you are. We're all bound to find ourselves in difficult situations, but we don't have to be bound *to* them. You're not a hostage to fear, pain, and doubt when you have hope, peace, and love in your corner. You were put right where you are by God on purpose. This wasn't some random accident. God is still with you, for you, and fighting for you, even when you can't see it.

The powerful part here is Paul *didn't* understand why he was placed there; it's not like God gave him some vision and told him why he was in prison. Instead, Paul prioritized his *obedience* to God, instead of trying to control the outcome. He realized that when you look at hardship as a way to glorify God, he gets glory every single time. And he understood that in his own control, the only thing he could do was obey God and trust him with the rest.

And so should we. The thing is, you *don't* have to understand the plan to trust that God has a purpose. Because if you truly did understand why something was happening, you wouldn't be walking by faith! You're not lost, not too far, not fallen away from God's will. You are *right* where he needs you. And there is a purpose even in the pain.

> For to me, to live is Christ, and to die is
> gain. But if I live on in the flesh, this will mean
> fruit from my labor; yet what I shall choose I

cannot tell. For I am hard-pressed between the two, having a desire to depart and be with Christ, which is far better. Nevertheless to remain in the flesh is more needful for you. And being confident of this, I know that I shall remain and continue with you all for your progress and joy of faith, that your rejoicing for me may be more abundant in Jesus Christ by my coming to you again. (vv. 21–26)

Paul goes on. He says, "I hope I will *never* be ashamed of Christ and I will continue to be bold. Because to me—living and dying are the same. If I live, awesome. I can preach to y'all. But if I die? Hallelujah! I'll be with my Lord and Savior. So it doesn't matter where I am or what I'm going through, I know all will be okay. I am not alone. I am not untouched. I am not lost.

"*I am not a hostage. Because to live is Christ and to die is gain. No outcome in this scenario is built for my downfall. While I'm here, I'm preaching the good news. And if something happens, so be it because then I'll be home with Jesus.*"

Even when you can't see a way, you can trust that he will make a way.

Maybe this sounds like your life right now. Just like Paul, you feel stuck behind bars, imprisoned to something you can't control. But when things become out of our control, that's an opportunity to give it up to the one who is in control. Let it all go. Don't worry about outcome; prioritize obedience. Because God is with you, for you, and has *promised* to make a way. So in the meantime, embrace the season you're in.

Because again, praising God when life is good is *easy*. Anyone can do that.

But a true sign of *really* knowing him intimately is continual praise, even when life gets tough. Because at that point, praise isn't just a single point in time but a consistent posture of surrender.

CHAPTER 4

Faithful on Purpose

Identifying Why

Question: What is your joy in the Lord?

Think about it. If you're a Christian today, chances are, there's a pretty big reason why you've decided to follow Christ. Nobody follows Jesus "just because." Either something has happened in your life or something spiritual has been understood by you to where you have fully committed the rest of your life to calling yourself a Christian. What's the point of being a Christ follower? Why do you love Jesus?

If the joy of the Lord is our strength (Nehemiah 8:10), what exactly is it? What is our joy in the Lord? Why is God good to you?

Well, for many of us today, it can be a number of things. Maybe your joy in the Lord is a blessing. At some point in your life, God has either provided for or given you something that has changed your life for the better. And because of that, you have decided since he has given something to you, you will give your life to him.

Or maybe your joy in the Lord is healing. You saw someone you love get healed miraculously, or maybe even, *you* experienced a miracle yourself. And because of that, you are so in awe of the Lord you have decided to believe there really is a God out there somewhere.

Or maybe, your joy in the Lord is spiritual exuberance. Believing in God makes you feel good, and when you sing the songs, you have rushes of excitement going through your veins. It's not so much that you deeply love God but more so that you love the feelings God can give you.

Those were kind of bizarre, so let's look at some more practical ones. Maybe your joy in the Lord is his goodness or his love or his forgiveness or his mercy, his provision, his faithfulness, his divinity, etc. Maybe, right now, your joy in the Lord is a good, spiritual reason that is understandable and relatable.

But remember—there's *got* to be more.

Do you see the common theme with all these? All these good reasons to follow Jesus are all based on *temporary events. God provided, so right now, I'm going to praise him. God loves me, so right now, I'll thank him. God forgives me, so right now, I'll feel good about myself.* All these reasons are temporary and based on a onetime feeling of excitement or realization of something beyond. And the problem is, when this spiritual high goes away, our joy in the Lord goes away as well.

But that's not how it's supposed to be. If the joy in the Lord is truly our strength, it must be something permanent, effective, and eternal. It can't be something that happens over and over again that leaves you empty in between cycles. Our joy in the Lord must be something that has happened already that has lasting effect on what's to come, providing permanent joy, no matter what we may be going through in life.

So—what is *really* our joy in the Lord? Paul tells us in 1 Corinthians 15, "O Death, where is your sting? O Hades, where is your victory? But thanks be to God, who gives us the victory through our Lord Jesus Christ" (vv. 55, 57).

If you want to experience a *true,* permanent joy in the Lord, it always has to go back to the greatest gift he's ever given—salvation. Through Jesus, we have access to eternal life and an invitation to a transformed heart. Why? Because on that cross, Jesus *eternally* saved us from sin and death forever! Death has no more victory and no more sting. And beyond the grave, there is everlasting life with the Father, awaiting our arrival.

This is true joy in the Lord. Remember what Habakkuk said, "Yet I will rejoice in the Lord, I will *joy* in the God of my *salvation*" (Habakkuk 3:18, italicization mine). Habakkuk realized that, no matter what he went through, there was always a reason to praise because of eternity. There was more to come. Even in the middle of complete catastrophe, he could still be joyful in the Lord because of something he's promised from the beginning—sending Jesus to save.

Our joy in the Lord should *always* be because of eternity and life beyond the grave. Why do we follow Jesus? Because he has saved us and granted us a new life *with* him for all of eternity. Choosing to rejoice in that is true joy because it can never go away; your salvation is always secure because he never changes.

There's always a reason to praise.

This overwhelming goodness should draw you closer to God's heart. God has *given* us a reason to rejoice in the permanent fact that Jesus rose from the grave. This life isn't the end; there is more to come and more intimacy to experience. And when you put heaven at the forefront of your faith, you drastically experience transformation.

Why? Because heaven is *final* and living with this eternal perspective connects you with him the way he's wanted all along.

The War in Your Mind

If we want to experience Jesus in a deep way, we have to connect the way we *think* to his thinking, too. Romans 12:2 says, "And do not be conformed to this world, but be transformed by the renewing of your mind, that you may prove what is that good and acceptable and perfect will of God." The New Living Translation says it like this: "Don't copy the behavior and customs of this world, but let God transform you into a new person by changing the way you *think*" (italicization mine). Obviously, if we want to know Jesus intimately, it starts by connecting our thoughts with his truth. Because with our mind, we will either be conformed to this world or transformed by his Spirit.

The way we think drastically affects the way we live. If you really think about it, our life is *always* moving in the direction of our strongest thoughts. If we are thinking negatively about ourselves, drowning in despair and shame, chances are, the choices we make will be based on that predetermined perception. On the other hand, if we truly believe we are forgiven and saved by grace, we will easily be able to tell by the way we live and how we treat people. The mind is powerful; Romans 8:5–6 says:

> For those who live according to the flesh set their minds on the things of the flesh, but those who live according to the Spirit, the things of the Spirit. For to be carnally minded is death, but to be spiritually minded is life and peace.

So often, today, we find ourselves drowned in the power of our own negative thinking. We allow our thoughts to determine how we live and give Satan a foothold in our mind, but it doesn't have to be this way. You can find new life in the power of Scripture and begin a new way of thinking, bringing you closer to Jesus at the same time. How? Because when you replace Satan's *lies* with Scripture's *truth,* you are giving the Word authority over your thoughts, not the devil. When you make the choice to take back your thoughts, you are allowing what *he* says about you to be the leading force of what you believe.

How does this affect us? Think about it. Let's identify lies Satan tells us that, over time, we start to believe and accept. *I don't feel loved, I can't be forgiven, I'm not good enough, I'll never know how to share my faith, I can't help others, I'm not good at serving, and I'm stuck in this one addiction. I'll always be a failure. God can't change me. I'm too far gone.* And over time, after repeating these thoughts over and over again, we begin to think they might actually be true—and we *believe* them. We allow Satan to dictate who we think we are because we don't fight back with what Christ says we are.

But today, all that ends. We are going to look at a specific way on how to fight the enemy's tactics and replace lies in our minds with God's Word.

We are going to create spiritual truths.

Second Corinthians 10:3–5 says:

> For though we walk in the flesh, we do not war according to the flesh. For the weapons of our warfare are not carnal but mighty in God for pulling down strongholds, casting down arguments and every high thing that exalts itself against the knowledge of God, bringing every thought into captivity to the obedience of Christ.

Maybe the intimacy you want with Jesus comes after you transform your thinking to what he really says about you. Maybe the deep, relational love you have yet to experience comes after embracing the truth of his Word. *This* is the power of spiritual truths, and the following examples are going to be a leading guide for you.

Never underestimate the power and authority of God's Word. Second Timothy 3:16–17 says:

> All Scripture is given by inspiration of God, and is profitable for doctrine, for reproof, for correction, for instruction in righteousness, that the man of God may be complete, thoroughly equipped for every good work.

The word here for "given by inspiration of God" is actually one word in Greek, *theä neustos*, which means "*God-breathed*." The literal word of God is directly from God himself, granting you the same power and authority that rose Christ from the dead. Think about that. We have access to God's very own breath to fight against our enemies and opposition—but we don't use it.

A spiritual truth is a Scripture-based declaration that affirms a new thought over a previous thought. You are taking God's Word and creating faith statements that highlight the truth about anything you are fighting against. Instead of believing the lies Satan has created on his own, you can *replace* them with rock-solid truth straight from the Bible. If we are going to be renewed in our minds, we must start planting some spiritual seeds.

- *Battling Anxiety*—Fear is not my master. I know God works all things for my good (Romans 8:28). I can be anxious for nothing and rejoice in his goodness, and Scripture promises his peace to surpass my own understanding (Philippians 4:6–7). I do not need to worry because tomorrow will take care of itself (Matthew 6:34). And if God is for me, nobody can be against me (Romans 8:31).

- *Battling Identity Belief*—I am saved by grace. And because works don't contribute to my salvation, I am not defined by my sin (Ephesians 2:8–9). No matter how far I run, I cannot escape God's love (Romans 8:38–39). I am defined by his scars, not my shame. Because I am in Christ, I am a brand-new creation (2 Corinthians 5:17). And if I confess my sin, every single time, he is faithful and just to forgive me and cleanse me from all unrighteousness (1 John 1:9).

- *Battling Temptation*—When I am tempted, God promises to give me a way out (1 Corinthians 10:13). He will not allow Satan to tempt me beyond what I can bear. If I am tempted, I am not fighting alone because greater is he in me than anyone else in the world (1 John 4:4). I am not a slave to sin—I am under no obligation to go back to my old ways (Romans 6:18). And I have a Savior who was put through the same tests and did not sin, so he can help me in my weakness (Hebrews 4:15, Hebrews 2:18).

- *Battling Spiritual Confidence*—I am fearfully and wonderfully made (Psalm 139:14). I am more than a conqueror (Romans 8:37). Christ in me is stronger than the wrong desires in me. I am Christ's ambassador, sent from heaven to earth for his glory (2 Corinthians 5:20). I am an overcomer by the blood of the Lamb (Revelation 12:11). And

I was created in God's own image when he formed me in my mother's womb (Genesis 1:26, Psalm 139:13).

✚ *Battling Trusting God*—I know that the Lord is my helper, and he will never leave me nor forsaken me (Hebrews 13:5–6). He is my shepherd through the valley, and he walks me through the valley of the shadow of death (Psalm 23:4). I can do all things through Christ who strengthens me (Philippians 4:13). And even if my flesh and heart may fail, the Lord is the strength of my heart and my portion forever (Psalm 73:26).

Do you see the power in Scripture? That fires me up! This is how we renew our mind. We replace the old lies with truth *straight* out of God's Word. And over time, as you continue to transform the way you think, God will transform the way you live. You don't have to be a slave to your thoughts because you can take them *captive* and center them on Christ.

If we are trying to get closer to Jesus, a big part of it is changing the way we think. Paul is clear in Galatians 6:7—"for whatever a man sows, that he will also reap." If you make the daily choice to renew your mind with Scripture, over time, you *will* see a change in your life. Be under the influence of the Spirit and make his thinking your thinking because you are always moving in the direction of your strongest thoughts.

You can win the war in your mind, create spiritual truths, make it personal, declare it, internalize it, write it down, memorize it, and, then, embrace the power of his Word. Do it over and over again until your thinking is transformed. Because if you *want* to grow closer to Jesus, your thinking has to be aligned with his Spirit and his truth.

In order to hear from God, you have to turn down the world's volume. Your life is always moving in the direction of your strongest thoughts.

Surrender

If you can recall at the beginning of the book, we highlighted a couple of major points that come with following Jesus. We talked about freedom, coming through God's abundant and overflowing grace. We also talked about relational intimacy, which comes from seeking him and how, in return, he will draw near to us. But there's one more word we listed that is most important out of all of them: *surrender*.

If you look at the Christian life, the main point is to have the faith to put aside what you think and desire and allow Christ to take over and lead. He is offering us something much bigger and better and is challenging us to let go of what we think and let him control the wheel. But reality is—that's extremely hard to do. With the sinful world we live in and a ferocious enemy we battle, finding true surrender is not easy. But if we really want to know Jesus in a deep and intimate way—surrender is the connecting piece. Because if we can grow to surrender our lives, we allow him to fill us up with his will and his way.

> Then Jesus said to His disciples, "If anyone desires to come after Me, let him deny himself, and take up his cross, and follow Me. For whoever desires to save his life will lose it, but whoever loses his life for My sake will find it." (Matthew 16:24–25)

If you want to be Jesus's disciple, he doesn't say you have to be perfect! Or to be his disciple, you have to have it all together! No, he says: *deny* yourself, take up the cross, and follow him—because if you try to save your own life and run your own show, you will surely lose it. Only when we give it up is where we truly find everlasting life.

Surrender isn't a onetime decision. Surrender is a daily choice.

Surrender isn't just a onetime all-time choice. Surrender is having the faith to give your life to the Lord every single day. It's a *daily* choice. And the faith challenge, as followers of Jesus, is to surrender everything—surrender your thoughts, surrender your feelings, surrender your will, surrender your wants.

Surrender your life.

Paul said in 1 Corinthians 15:31 that he "dies *daily.*" Daily! Every single day, Paul must choose, by faith, to surrender his life to God. Because if we think we can just pass by every day without acknowledging our surrender, we will fall right back into the trap we started with—no trust, no faith, no submission. We'll try to do life *our* way, which always ends in losing it (see verse 25 again above).

Why is this important? Because if we want to experience God as our provider, deliverer, and director, we must let *him* control the reins. But with that comes a serious step back and a serious commitment to trust through the unknown.

Represent

Whose story does your life tell?

Think about it. *Really* think about it. And don't just say "Jesus" because it sounds right. Who are you representing? Who are you *really* representing? When you walk into a room. What you wear. What you post on social media. How you interact with people. How you treat others. How passionate you are to reach people. How you love. How you serve. How you forgive.

Who are you *really* representing? Because as much as I want to sit here and tell you that I represent Jesus all the time, so often, I find myself only representing me. *Is this good enough for you? Do you approve of me? See how good I am?* But the thing is, as Christians who are servants of Jesus, we are called to represent him.

If you step back for a minute and *really* think about it—we aren't the main characters here. God doesn't exist for us. We exist to serve him. Yet so often, we begin to believe the lie that our lives are about our story and our worth. And if we live life thinking we're the top priority, we don't give Jesus the center stage he deserves.

This all ties back into the topic of surrender. When you represent Jesus, you are completely surrendering your life to his will and his kingdom. Your life is no longer about you. Your life is about doing his work, led by his Spirit, driven by his power. It's all him. And *surrender* in this aspect is completely letting go of *your* story and letting your life reflect his.

The good news? Surrender always brings revival. When we surrender, we replace our plans with his, upgrading our wants and desires with eternal purposes—out with the old, in with the new. Your life is no longer about how much you can make and how much you can acquire but, rather, how much he can do *through* you to impact eternity. Surrender is a big deal. And we're going to see how Paul illustrates this perspective wholeheartedly.

In Acts 20, Paul is in the middle of a mission's journey in Ephesus. And the good news is, he was thriving there. Paul was relating to the people and faithfully spreading the Word of God. Paul was *comfortable* there. But God was calling him somewhere else.

Paul had a choice. He could fight for what he wanted and what he thought was best—or he could surrender and obey God.

> And see, now I go bound in the spirit to Jerusalem, not knowing the things that will happen to me there, except that the Holy Spirit testifies in every city, saying that chains and tribulations await me. But none of these things move me; nor do I count my life dear to myself, so that I may finish my race with joy, and the ministry which I received from the Lord Jesus, to testify to the gospel of the grace of God. (Acts 20:22–24)

What did Paul do? Paul realized his life was not his own but the Lord's. By faith, he trusted that if he would just listen to the Spirit, he would end up right where God needed him to be. Paul counted his life as worth *nothing*. Nothing! *My life means nothing to me, except to do the work of God.* This huge faith statement is a picture-perfect example of surrender. Paul could have very easily done things his way. *Things are going well here in Ephesus. The people love me, God's Word is being preached, what else could I ask for? I mean, this is easy. I'm a fan favorite here.* But instead, he gave up what *he* thought was supposed to happen and let God route his course. Paul stepped out of the driver seat and didn't care about any obstacles on the road.

This is the position of surrender we need to get to. We live in such a self-centered world that focuses only on how much we can attain. We're taught to show ourselves off, promote ourselves, and highlight only our bests for people to see what we want them to see. But if you're a follower of Jesus, it doesn't have to be that way. Not only is your identity already in Christ but the more you try to *save* your life by your own efforts, the more you're actually losing it. Surrender doesn't chase after anything. Surrender lets God direct you from the throttle.

Will it be easy? Not a chance! Calling always costs. If your greatest gift isn't also your greatest burden, you probably aren't doing it right. But the cost of following Jesus is *always* worth it in the end. Look at these four points we see in Paul's surrender choice:

- ✠ *Spirit Prompting*—If you are walking by the Spirit, opening your heart to his will and his work, you will feel compelled, led, and directed to do things. Now, this isn't something you were hoping for or planning. This is a divine direction where you just *feel* God calling you to do something out of the ordinary, totally unknown. Paul said he was *compelled* to go to Jerusalem; he was drawn and led by the Spirit. He wasn't in control of the outcome. He simply obeyed. It may be a big assignment, or it may be a little one—but every prompting from God holds the same divine importance.
  Choose obedience over outcome.
- ✠ *Certain Uncertainty*—If you do feel a prompting, you will feel led by the Spirit to do something, and then, that's about it—no details, no extra information, no exact blueprint. Paul said he was going to Jerusalem, *not knowing* what would happen to him there. He had no clue. Didn't know the final page and didn't know any details. God needs to lead you step-by-step because if he showed you everything, you never would have the faith to take

the first step. Be certain that there will be uncertainty—because if you never live with any uncertainty, you are not living by faith.

- *Predictable Resistance*—If you are following a divine pathway from God, expect spiritual opposition. Paul was ready—he knew for sure there was prison and hardship coming, but he remembered his greater reward. If you are not ready for spiritual opposition *for* God, you are not ready to be used *by* God. There will always be spiritual opposition. Embrace it. There is a spiritual enemy who does *not* want you fulfilling God's call on your life, and you have to be ready for it.

  Criticism is the confirmation of calling.

- *Uncommon Confidence*—Go back to Paul's surrender statement: "Nor do I count my life dear to myself." His life meant nothing. *My only desire is to serve the Lord Jesus and testify about the good grace of God. My only aim is to finish the race.* That sounds pretty confident, doesn't it? Think about Paul. He was a faithful Jesus follower who endured hardship, opposition, and oppression. He didn't plan this. He prioritized obedience. And in the end, his faithfulness far outweighed any achievement he had in life. He said in 2 Timothy 4:7, "I have fought the good fight, I have finished the race, I have kept the faith." Paul couldn't see into the future. Paul was only worried about his obedience *today.* He knew God was with him, for him, and in him wherever he went, and that confidence led him to complete submission and surrender.

I personally think surrender is the hardest challenge for the everyday Christian. Naturally, we want our will to be done because we think we know enough. But no matter how much we think we know, we will never be able to fulfill the divine plan God has already prepared on our own. Give up your life, take up your cross, and just follow him. Because he has *promised* to save your life when you lose it and he wants to use you in big, eternal ways.

But he can't use you when you're running your own show.

There's Nothing Better

We live in a world that is endlessly pursuing *more*.

Think about it. Think about the people we interact with—the celebrities we idolize, the social media influencers, our coaches, our coworkers, our bosses, our friends, our teachers, our families, our siblings, *ourselves*.

We are always chasing *more*—more power, more performance, more improvement, more comfort, more materials, more money, more fame, more accomplishment, more acknowledgment, more appreciation, more followers, more happiness.

We always want *more*. But the problem is, we are looking for an answer from a world that cannot provide a solution. Think back to the very beginning of this book. What was I also searching for? *More.* We all do it, and rightfully so. We were *created* to experience more, but we look for it in the wrong things.

Sometimes, we get so caught up in the rush of life that we put aside our pursuit to know and love Jesus intimately. We pursue the wrong things in life when Jesus is offering more right here. We seek satisfaction in things that truly cannot satisfy, forgetting that God has had more for you to experience all along.

I got stuck in this cycle big-time as I went through my younger years. Being surrounded by a culture that promotes nothing but a want for more, naturally, I birthed this desire to be the best and attain the most. My life was no longer about people and purpose, but my priorities changed to power and position. I cared so much about where I was and who all knew me that I completely forgot about the biggest piece of my life—Jesus.

Being an athlete didn't help either. All my life, promotion of self was preached everywhere I went. *Prove yourself. Make them regret not taking a chance on you. Show them what you can do. Be the best.* And after falling under the influence of these voices, my life's goal shifted from contentment in Christ to chasing after a goal I could never achieve—gaining man's approval.

I was running in a race with no winner.

Until finally—Jesus broke me. Like he *broke* me to a point of complete surrender and obedience to him. My entire perspective and view on life changed after realizing what he wanted all along. My goal isn't to make it big. My goal is to know Jesus. And every single day, my priority is to know *him* as deep and intimate as I can. I'm not trying to be better today at anything. I'm just trying to know Jesus. That's it! I'm not trying to finish, accomplish, or achieve anything. I am choosing to live in grace and love in truth. It's a mindset and an intention of the heart—what God has longed for the entire time.

This needs to be our faith statement: In everything I do, my first and foremost priority is to seek Jesus in it. Everywhere I go, everyone I talk to, everything I see, every conversation I have—I want to seek Jesus. Because the more we prioritize seeing Jesus in everyday life, the more we will see his glory in all of it. If the goal is to know him deeply and intimately, it starts and ends with seeing him through everything he has created.

A true faith statement says my life is not about me and my journey. My life is about getting to know Jesus. And everything that happens in between is preparing and introducing me to a new way to know him and experience him. I'm not worried about the outcome of my life because I trust the one in control. *I'm prioritizing spending every day I live chasing after Jesus.*

Don't chase after things that don't matter and don't last. Don't waste months, years of your life running after a crown that holds no eternal significance. Don't waste a day! Choose to see and know Jesus now—today. Because he is offering so much more than this world can, and it will never be taken away.

In everything I do, my goal is to know Jesus. I deeply desire to know him intimately, so I will look for him constantly. It all goes back to the word we've highlighted all along: *abiding*.

> Do you not know that those who run in a race all run, but one receives the prize? Run in such a way that you may obtain it. And everyone who competes for the prize is temperate in

all things. Now they do it to obtain a perishable crown, but we for an imperishable crown. (1 Corinthians 9:24–25)

Lord, I Look to You

I want to close this chapter out with a big faith challenge.

Step back for a moment. Think about what we *go* to God for—our requests, our prayers, our intentions, etc. Think just for a moment behind the *why* we go to God for, when we do. Because if we're being honest, sometimes, we go to God for reasons with no substance, lacking real faith and reverence for him.

What do I mean? Think about the prayers we pray. *Lord, keep me safe. Please don't let me go through this tough time. Sure, I know it was designed for me to draw closer to you, but I don't feel like experiencing that type of hurt.* Instead of asking God to comfort us *through* the storm, we ask him to take it away completely! Without any sort of deep relationship or connection, we look to God as someone who can answer all of our requests—not someone we deeply love and respect.

In all our intentions, we need to be more bothered by our *sin* than our desire for blessings or deliverance. Should we have faith that God can tear down a prison wall in our life? Absolutely. But if you *really* want to experience him in a deep and intimate way, put all *your* worries to the side and think about what his will warrants. He wants to *know* you intimately. And we should be bothered more by our lack of commitment than asking him to just give us what we want.

How can this be? The only way you can come to this point of obedience is *surrender*. You must surrender all your current thoughts, feelings, and emotions to prioritize God's will and God's priorities alone. Praise isn't a circumstantial action; it's a posture of life. And if we can get to a spot where our praise is evident and permanent, solely based on his goodness alone, we can break through this shallow-water Christianity we all want to swim away from.

Your prayers? Focused on abiding. Your praises? Constant. Your worship? Continual. Your wants and desires? Centered on Jesus. All your actions and disciplines are centered around experiencing him more, not *receiving* more from him. It's a faith choice that puts God's presence in higher demand over God's presents. Yeah. I went there.

Imagine you're in the middle of a huge worship setting. Thousands of people on fire for Christ. Voices from every corner are singing praises to the one who is worthy. I think about moments like this all the time. In that very moment—Christ is enough for me. After singing about his goodness and glory, in that *very* moment, he is enough. Nothing else matters, and nothing else can satisfy. His *goodness* is enough for me. I wouldn't need anything else in this world to change how I feel right then about Jesus. *In his power alone I stand.*

The same question raises once more: Is he *enough* for you? Is his goodness, glory, power, and might enough to satisfy your weary soul? Or do you need *something else* from him to qualify him as good? Paul said it in 2 Corinthians 12:9 while battling his thorn in the flesh: "And [God] said to me, 'My grace is sufficient for you, for My strength is made perfect in weakness.'" The question stands alone. Is his *grace* enough for you? Is his goodness, faithfulness, mercy, love— is it all enough for you? Because if it is, his power can strengthen your weakness. And you can experience never-ending permanent good- ness in the presence of a good God.

Change your perspective. That's the challenge for you today. Is God good for what he does? Or is he good for who he is? Is Christ enough for you? Are you sufficed in his love? Because if you are, Scripture promises you *won't lack a thing* (Psalm 23:1). And if you can find peace and promise in his character, you will maintain it, no matter what circumstance you go through. Because at that point, God is good, period. And what Jesus did on that cross far outweighs anything we may face or go through today.

If you feel convicted by the Spirit to change your perspective and have a longing, desire to experience *more* in your relationship with Jesus, talk to him about it. King David said in Psalm 139:23– 24, "Search me, O God, and know my heart; try me, and know my anxieties; and see if there is any wicked way in me, and lead me in the way everlasting." When we ask the Lord to point out something in us that isn't of him, he promises to reveal it to us. But notice also what the psalmist says in verse 24: "See if there is any wicked way in me." David wasn't praying for God to bless him; he trusted that God would supply all his needs. David was praying for God to *reveal* to him ways in his heart that were keeping him back from experiencing him fully.

And we should do the exact same.

If you feel deeply compelled to pray a prayer like David did, you can use this as a guide:

Lord, I pray that you search my heart completely. Reveal to me anything in me that is not of or from you. Make me more bothered by my sin than my desire for blessings and lead me in the way everlasting for the rest of my life. Help me to treasure your presence more than any present you can ever give. Jesus is enough for me.

In Jesus's name, amen.

CHAPTER 5

Following Jesus

He Is—

So far, we've gone over what God has wanted all along—a deep, intimate relationship with each of his beloved children. We've also talked about *how* he molds us into everything he has created us to be. We've gone over intention, transformation, and surrender, but this chapter is going to focus on one thing: Jesus's way of life. Obviously, we all know what Scripture *says* about Jesus, but to look at the way he actually *lived* and the values he held has a drastic effect on how we live today. If our aim is to know Jesus in an intimate way, we must know who he was and how he carried himself in everyday life. Our key verse for this first section is John 14:6, which says, "Jesus said to him, 'I am the way, the truth, and the life. No one comes to the Father except through Me.'"

The Way

If Jesus, first and foremost, is the *way*, in what way did Jesus live? If you look throughout Scripture, the common theme we see is Jesus lived with *ease*. Now, he didn't battle sin with ease—that's not the context here. Jesus lived his life with ease—never rushing, never becoming anxious, and never becoming burdened by what was going on around him.

Something we don't do very well.

Think about the way we live today. We run around like headless chickens to our next event, gathering, activity, you name it. We live in such a *rushed* world. But if Jesus was never rushed, neither should we.

Mark 2:13–14 briefly describes:

> Then He went out again by the sea; and all the multitude came to Him, and He taught them. As He passed by, He saw Levi the son of Alphaeus sitting at the tax office. And He said to him, "Follow Me." So he arose and followed Him.

Jesus *passed by*. He wasn't in a rush. Jesus was chillin'. Never in Scripture will you ever find Jesus running—*Jesus sprinted to the dead man. Jesus raced to the mute*—never. Jesus was on his own time because he trusted the one in charge of time. He may have been busy. But he was *never* in a rush.

And we see that. He said to Levi, "Follow Me," and Levi did. He saw the way Jesus lived and fell out of bondage immediately. Because Jesus is not a what-have-you-done-for-me-lately kind of Savior. He is one that provides rest and ease through the trials of this life.

Let's get even more specific. Mark 5 tells another story about Jesus on the way to heal a young girl. Jairus, a synagogue leader, came up to Jesus and begged him to heal his dying daughter, so Jesus agreed. The only problem was, on the way there—Jesus was stopped.

> Now a certain woman had a flow of blood for twelve years, and had suffered many things from many physicians. She had spent all that she had and was no better, but rather grew worse. When she heard about Jesus, she came behind Him in the crowd and touched His garment. For

> she said, "If only I may touch His clothes, I shall be made well." (vv. 25–28)

> And Jesus, immediately knowing in Himself that power had gone out of Him, turned around in the crowd and said," Who touched My clothes? (v. 30)

> But the woman, fearing and trembling, knowing what had happened to her, came and fell down before Him and told Him the whole truth. And He said to her, "Daughter, your faith has made you well. Go in peace, and be healed of your affliction. (vv. 33–34)

Think about this. Imagine yourself in Jesus's time. You have a dying family member, and you see how quickly their body has become more and more weary over the past couple of days. So you think of Jesus, someone who can heal, and hurry to ask him for help. Time is running out. We don't have a moment to spare.

You finally get to Jesus, and he agrees to help. He'll come and heal them. But the only problem is, on the way to *your* miracle, he stops and heals someone else. Jesus is *not* in a rush to heal your loved one.

And Jairus felt that. Scripture says:

> While He was still speaking, some came from the ruler of the synagogue's house who said, "Your daughter is dead. Why trouble the Teacher any further?" As soon as Jesus heard the word that was spoken, He said to the ruler of the synagogue, "Do not be afraid; only believe." (Mark 5:35–36)

It's too late. Your daughter is dead. Don't bother him anymore.
But Jesus says no. Don't be afraid. Don't rush. Just believe. And he healed her (v. 42).

How often do we do this in our own lives? Almost out of control, we run around town and live our lives on the go because we feel like we don't have time. We're too busy—too busy for people, too busy for relationships, too busy for prayer, too busy for Scripture, too busy for service, too busy for community—

Too busy for God. Because the *speed* of this world has overwhelmed our own spiritual clock of rest.

God didn't create you to always be on the go. He created you to be sustained in the peace he offers. You were not designed to live a rushed and busy life. You were created to experience the same resurrection power and ease that Jesus granted you when he died on that cross.

So what's the solution? How can we find freedom from the bondage of busyness? The solution is not that we need more time. The solution is we need more of what matters *most*. That's it. You don't need more time. You need more time with what matters most or *who* matters most.

You need more time with God.

And he has *promised* you rest. Matthew 11:28–30 says:

> Come to Me, all you who labor and are heavy laden, and I will give you rest. Take My yoke upon you and learn from Me, for I am gentle and lowly in heart, and you will find rest for your souls. For My yoke is easy and My burden is light.

What is a yoke? A yoke is used as a control piece for two farm animals. This piece would go around each of their necks so that when one animal moved, the other had to move also. Or in the same way, if one animal did not move, the other one didn't move either. It was a way to control the pace of which *both* animals moved as one, often used when they would walk through fields.

So what is Jesus saying? Very plainly, Jesus is *inviting* you to join his yoke. He is reaching out with open arms, wanting you to walk so close to him you can't escape his grip. Because if you take his yoke and cling to him more than ever, you will find yourself approaching and accepting life's scenarios much differently. You will have peace. You will find joy. You will live for purpose. All because you are basically *tied* to the one who gives all of those anyway.

The good news? His burden is light—it costs you nothing. All you have to do is accept this invitation of intimacy where he not only leads you but walks right beside you. He is not only *showing* you another way, but you now have access to walk *alongside* the way. His yoke is easy, and his burden is light.

Maybe this feels like you and your life. You're always on the run, always on the go. And you feel this longing, desire to slow down and really experience peace. I encourage you to take his yoke. Jesus doesn't want you to battle life alone. He has offered a place near his yoke, where you have access to learn the way directly from *the way* himself. Take it.

Because Jesus may have been busy, but he was never in a rush. And if we are going to follow the *way* of which he lived, we shouldn't be in a rush either.

The Truth

"And you shall know the truth, and the truth shall make you free" (John 8:32).

Understand this point: Knowing truth provides freedom.

The more you genuinely *know* truth, the more you can be set free. Truth is real, and truth is a person! Scripture says that in the beginning was the Word, and the Word was God (John 1:1). So the more we can unlock and embrace what truth is and what truth does, the more we can find freedom in this physical life from sin.

Step back for a minute. Why did Jesus come? What purpose was he to serve? John 3:17 says, "For God did not send His Son into the world to condemn the world, but that the world through Him might be saved." Jesus came for one reason—to save the world. What does that mean? It means Jesus was born to die. The only way he could save us was to sacrifice himself for our sins, and with that came a heavy cost.

How did he do it? How could he mentally take in everything he was about to face and experience? Because of one reason: Jesus prioritized eternal life over the physical one. That's the truth! Jesus cared way more about eternity in heaven than the temporary life he had on earth. And if he prioritized eternity, we should too.

Thinking with an eternal perspective can set you free. Through the power of the Spirit, the more you set your sights on heaven, the more you can experience God and his eternal love. Colossians 3:2 says, "Set your mind on things of heaven, not of earth." The more you think eternally, the better you can connect with your heavenly Father. Don't believe me? Let's prove it in Scripture.

Here are four big points that come with thinking eternally:

Thinking eternally gives us clarity on why we are here.

When you think eternally, you begin to understand purpose. How? You understand that the *focus* of your life isn't even this one but the next. Your first and foremost priority is heaven.

Think about Jesus's life and everything he did. Although he already had access to the throne of glory, he still prioritized eternity in everything he said and did. Jesus loved, forgave, embraced, encouraged, ministered—all because he lived with an eternal perspective. How? Because on a regular day, your flesh does not incline you toward those things. On an ordinary day, we don't feel like bearing fruit of the Spirit. But when you think eternally, you understand it's not just something you can do but something you are called to do.

Paul also understood this. Recall his big faith statement in Acts 20:

> And see, now I go bound in the spirit to Jerusalem, not knowing the things that will happen to me there, except that the Holy Spirit testifies in every city, saying that chains and tribulations await me. But none of these things move me; nor do I count my life dear to myself, so that

> I may finish my race with joy, and the ministry
> which I received from the Lord Jesus, to testify to
> the gospel of the grace of God. (vv. 22–24)

Paul counted his life as *nothing* but to share the good news of God. That was his only purpose. How could he possibly surrender his life in such a way? Because he thought eternally. He put eternal souls won over temporary moments that could be experienced. He bypassed all of it, solely because he had experienced the grace of God himself and had no desire but to share it with others.

Thinking eternally gives you purpose.

Thinking eternally unlocks God's divine will.

Matthew 16 tells a story of Jesus talking to Peter before his crucifixion. Jesus is telling the disciples that he will be crucified but raised on the third day. However, Peter, thinking he knows better than Jesus, got mad at him for saying such a thing. Peter rebuked Jesus for thinking it would be a good thing for him to die in such a way.

> From that time Jesus began to show to His disciples that He must go to Jerusalem, and suffer many things from the elders and chief priests and scribes, and be killed, and be raised the third day. Then Peter took Him aside and began to rebuke Him, saying, "Far be it from You, Lord; this shall not happen to You!" But He turned and said to Peter, "Get behind Me, Satan! You are an offense to Me, for you are not mindful of the things of God, but the things of men." (Matthew 16:21–23)

Jesus calls Peter Satan because he can't understand the eternal purpose of something that's happening. See that in the story? Jesus *scolds* Peter for only seeing things from man's point of view and not God's.

If Peter thought eternally here, he would have seen the eternal benefit of salvation through physical hardship. But because he only thought about what happens *right now,* he couldn't see through to what Jesus was saying. We do this all the time. We only think about what we are doing now without realizing God is using it for a greater purpose later—one that will impact the kingdom.

Isaiah 55:8–9 says:

> "For My thoughts are not your thoughts, nor are your ways My ways," says the Lord. "For as the heavens are higher than the earth, so are My ways higher than your ways, and My thoughts than your thoughts."

God's will is not something you can just accept. It takes eternal thinking, and it takes the Spirit's help to discern and understand what he is doing. But you will never unlock God's will if you are only thinking about the present.

Thinking eternally motivates you to a life of holiness.

When you think eternally and see grace as a freedom from sin, you begin to see there really is a way out from unrighteousness. Let's look at some things Jesus did throughout his life. Jesus fasted for forty days out in the wilderness. He totally ignored Satan when he tried to tempt him. He didn't have bitterness just sitting in his heart because of the Pharisees. He never sinned. He *willfully* bore the cross and followed God's will. How? How could he do such a thing? Because when you think eternally, your first and foremost priority is to glorify your Father with your life.

Jonathan Edwards said, "A true and faithful Christian does not make holy living an accidental thing. It's their greatest concern. As the business of a soldier is to fight, so the business of the Christian is to be like Christ." When you think about eternity and the life we will live once we get there, the first thought should always be holy living. *I don't deserve heaven, I deserve hell. I'm a sinner. But Jesus died for me while I was stuck in sin. And because I have eternal life through him and him alone, I am going to make it my greatest concern to live my life in a way that was worth dying for.*

Paul said this in Galatians 2: "For I through the law died to the law that I might live to God" (v. 19). Remember, grace is not an excuse to sin—it's a freedom not to. But the only way you will find a desire to honor grace is to think eternally about the Savior who gave it to you in the first place.

Thinking eternally provides hope for what's to come.

Jesus says this in John 14:

> Let not your heart be troubled; you believe in God, believe also in Me. In My Father's house are many mansions; if it were not so, I would have told you. I go to prepare a place for you. And if I go and prepare a place for you, I will come again and receive you to Myself; that where I am, there you may be also. And where I go you know, and the way you know. (vv. 1–4)

Jesus has prepared a *place* for you in heaven. How cool is that! There's a mansion in glory waiting where he will meet you there, not because of anything good you have done but because of his great love and mercy.

We all face tough times. Chances are, you are either going through a storm, just entered a storm, or about to face one. Life is hard. But there is a promise Scripture offers when we let heaven be our hope for what's to come. Romans 8:18 says, "For I consider that the sufferings of this present time are not worthy to be compared with the glory which shall be revealed in us." The battle is already won. Jesus said it is finished (John 19:30). There is glory coming, and heaven is awaiting. Let eternity be your hope. Because the more you think about the glory to come, the easier it will be to endure the suffering you are facing now.

"If we endure hardship, we will also reign with him" (2 Timothy 2:12).

The truth is, thinking eternally can provide freedom. And if Jesus prioritized heaven over earth, we should do the same thing.

What you believe about eternity determines how you will live today.

The Life

Real life begins when Jesus becomes the source of it.

Lastly, Jesus came to give and speak life to everyone who was around him. Recall our verse at the beginning of the book: "I have come that they may have life, and that they may have it more abundantly" (John 10:10). Obviously, from what he is saying, there is *something* that Jesus carries with him that far surpasses life as we know it—something that holds more value to the point of where he calls it *abundant*.

Jesus didn't come just to improve your physical life. Jesus came to *save* your eternal one.

He came to introduce eternity. He came to set the captive free from all bondage and slavery. That's why he is the life. I mean, think about it. What did Jesus do so well that spread life so abundantly? Jesus was a kingdom speaker, a gospel empoweree, a life-giving, abundant-loving, grace-seeking, mercy-fulfilling Savior. Jesus lived for the people and represented all that God is in the flesh. He looked at *every* encounter with someone as a way to bring home a lost soul to salvation. Like a shepherd running after his sheep, Jesus left the ninety-nine every time to find the lost one.

And if we are followers of Christ, we should do the same.

Mark 2 describes a story of a man who was paralyzed and brought to Jesus. But he wasn't just brought to Jesus—he was *forced* to him. This man had four friends that were willing to do anything to get their friend to Jesus. In fact, they even tore through a roof to get to him (v. 4).

And when they could not come near Him because of the crowd, they uncovered the roof where He was. So when they had broken through, they let down the bed on which the paralytic was lying. When Jesus saw their faith, He said to the paralytic," Son, your sins are forgiven. (vv. 4–5)

"But that you may know that the Son of Man has power on earth to forgive sins"—He said to the paralytic, "I say to you, arise, take up your bed, and go to your house." Immediately he arose, took up the bed, and went out in the presence of them all, so that all were amazed and glorified God, saying, "We never saw anything like this!" (vv. 10–12)

Understand the context of the story here. Jesus is in a room full of people—some religious teachers and some regular townsmen. And then suddenly, dropping from a roof, four men and their friend come flying in, hoping Jesus can heal the paralytic. And notice the *very first* thing Jesus says to this man who could not walk: "*Son, your sins are forgiven.*"

Imagine. Imagine being paralyzed all your life. Imagine not knowing if or when you would ever walk for the first time. And after hearing about someone who could heal you and you finally get to him, he doesn't even tell you to get up and walk. The first thing he says to you is your sins are *forgiven*.

You can see where Jesus's priorities were. Yes, he could heal, and yes, he cares about your physical life. But his first and foremost priority is saving your soul eternally. And this story is a clear representative of how much Jesus prioritizes eternal security over something else in this temporary, physical life.

In everything Jesus did, his priority was to populate heaven. He didn't just heal, love, and forgive then leave it at that. Jesus introduced them to new life beyond the grave. If eternity is the only place where there is life and life abundantly, Jesus made that his first and foremost priority. He came to seek, find, and save lost souls. And if we are trying to follow Jesus, we should be doing the same.

As Christians, our job isn't to just live after we've secured eternity. Our goal is to make sure others are ready too. We were created to *thrive* spiritually and spread the joy we feel to everyone else around us. Jesus told this parable in Luke 15:

> What man of you, having a hundred sheep, if he loses one of them, does not leave the ninety-nine in the wilderness, and go after the one which is lost until he finds it? And when he has found it, he lays it on his shoulders, rejoicing. And when he comes home, he calls together his friends and neighbors, saying to them, "Rejoice with me, for I have found my sheep which was lost!" I say to you that likewise there will be more joy in heaven over one sinner who repents than over ninety-nine just persons who need no repentance. (Luke 15:4–7)

Who is the shepherd in this story? It's Jesus. Jesus *is* the shepherd. And he is willing to leave *everyone* and *everything* behind in pursuit of just one lost sheep. So if you are a follower of Jesus, you should be doing the same.

Your life, mission, and duty as a follower of Jesus is to do what Jesus does. He hunts down the lost sheep. He leaves *everything* valuable to him just to seek the one lost heart that needs saving. Because you never know what could happen and you never know the power of your testimony and discipleship. Through Jesus, as you walk and follow him, you have the power to impact someone's life and even better their eternity.

Jesus was your shepherd. Still is. But now, it's your time to leave the ninety-nine and find the one. By the power of the Spirit, it's time to not just be the one found but to seek the one to find.

Because if Jesus is the life and we are trying to follow Jesus, we should be doing the same.

Send Me

All my life, I've been told my job as a Christian was to share my faith. Growing up in the church, I heard daily how we need to be constantly looking for people in need of faith, hope, and love. But the problem was, as a young kid, I really didn't have any *motivation* for spreading the gospel. Not only was it really uncomfortable and hard to do but I just didn't have any passion for going out of my way and being encouraged enough to tell others about Jesus.

Maybe this sounds like you. You've grown up in the church, and you've been a Christian for most of your life. But the problem is, you don't see a *need* for spreading the gospel. Someone else will do it. It's not *your* calling to bear. It's way too uncomfortable. And over time, after not acting upon a command we have been given to disciple others, you've found yourself stuck in a pit with absolutely no spiritual enthusiasm.

How? How do you find motivation for advancing the gospel? How can you wake up every day with the same fire inside you to spread the good news? This is your key point: you must be *so* overwhelmed by his grace that you have no other choice but to surrender.

You must be so thankful for what God has done for you that your *only* intention is to tell someone else about it. That's it. You will only find a passion for sharing the goodness of God when you have experienced the goodness of God yourself. And if you have truly been transformed by the redemptive power of grace, you will do anything short of sin to show others the freedom and love that comes with it.

This cause and effect is the best way to find spiritual passion. *I'm a sinner, but Jesus died for me. And because he died for me, I am set free from all bondage to sin and shame. I don't deserve a lick of grace, but because he freely gave it, I have radical joy. And because I have so much joy, I have no other desire but to share and introduce it with others.* We're going to look at an Old Testament story found in Isaiah 6 that reflects this principle so clearly. And as we read through it, identify the shift in Isaiah's heart as he finally discovers the overwhelming love and mercy of the Lord.

The story picks up as a vision Isaiah has in heaven:

> In the year that King Uzziah died, I saw the Lord sitting on a throne, high and lifted up, and the train of His robe filled the temple. Above it stood seraphim; each one had six wings: with two he covered his face, with two he covered his feet, and with two he flew. And one cried to another and said: "Holy, holy, holy is the Lord of hosts; the whole earth is full of His glory!" (Isaiah 6:1–3)

Isaiah was in the presence of God, surrounded by angels who were singing praises to him. It was a literal picture of heaven. But Isaiah felt ashamed for his sins. He realized he was in a holy location, but he, in fact, was unholy.

Isaiah *recognized* his sin.

"Woe is me, for I am undone! Because I am a man of unclean lips, and I dwell in the midst of a people of unclean lips; for my eyes have seen the King, the Lord of hosts" (Isaiah 6:5).

Woe is me! Because of his shame, he thought he was doomed, no longer able to be used by God. Isaiah connected his sin to his basis of discipleship. He thought he was too far gone. But watch:

> Then one of the seraphim flew to me, having in his hand a live coal which he had taken with the tongs from the altar. And he touched my mouth with it, and said: "Behold, this has touched your lips; your iniquity is taken away, and your sin purged" (Isaiah 6:6–7)

Isaiah, you are forgiven. Your guilt is removed. Sins are purged. You are *brand-new.*

But then, look what happens next. Watch the immediate shift for Isaiah:

"Also I heard the voice of the Lord, saying: 'Whom shall I send, and who will go for Us?' Then I said, 'Here am I! Send me'" (Isaiah 6:8).

God asks a very clear question: who wants to work for me? Who wants to serve me well? Who wants to represent my kingdom?

Then Isaiah says, "God, I'm ready. *Send me.*"

What happened? Isaiah realized the truth—that God was so good and his grace so great he had no other desire *but* to serve. Isaiah was motivated. Motivated by the saving of his sin to be the *very* first one to go when God asked.

Notice the shift in Isaiah's perspective in this story. This true reflection of a repentant heart is the basis of saving faith. R. Kent Hughes is quoted as saying, "Repentance is the telltale mark of the grace of God in a Christian's life. Saving faith and true repentance are always found together. Saved souls are repentant souls." In other words, to *really* know you've been transformed by the grace of God, your first step will be longing for repentance and desire to live a transformed life. Does that mean perfection? Not at all. It only reflects an immediate turnaround and change—something we see here with Isaiah.

This is how you light that spiritual fire you've always wanted. Let your redemption be the driving factor in your discipleship. Because if you have truly been radically transformed by the goodness and grace of God, you will feel an overwhelming sense of joy and gratitude. And if this joy is the leading factor in your life, you will have no other desire but to share it with someone else.

Lord, help me to be so enthused by your love that I value nothing else but to share it with others.

"Send me."

True Calling

"For we are His workmanship, created in Christ Jesus for good works, which God prepared beforehand that we should walk in them" (Ephesians 2:10).

And the good news is, God has already *prepared* a way for you to work—you just have to embrace it. See, as Christians, we always hear about purpose and calling and are told that our lives are to be used for big things. But the problem is, we are never told *how* or *what* to do. We have this desire to serve God in a big way, but we barely have any idea where to start.

If you're a Christian, you understand this world is *not* your home. First Peter 2:11 says we are "temporary residents and foreigners" to this world. We are just passing through. And just as Jesus sought after us to save us for all of eternity, we should be doing the exact same for other people in need.

Now, this is where it gets tricky. Because after hearing all of that, I'm sure you're feeling *burdened*. It's *your* job. *You* must save thousands. *You* have to minister to every person you see. *You're* the one doing all the work here.

The church today never really explains the entire story. Yes, our lives are to be used for kingdom purposes, and yes, we are to reflect Jesus to everyone around us. But if you look at Scripture, you'll see that the *number one* duty for a Christian is not to save people—it's to know and become more like Jesus.

"[God] has saved us and *called* us with a *holy calling*, not according to our works, but according to His own purpose and grace which was given to us in Christ Jesus before time began" (2 Timothy 1:9, italicization mine).

All the pressure is off. Your calling as a Christian is *not* to save thousands and minister to millions. That's not your responsibility. Your calling is to become more and more like Jesus, understanding and experiencing God's grace in new and radical ways. And then, as we talked about before, the more you surrender and allow Jesus to transform you, the more he will work through you to reach other people.

This is the big point: your calling isn't a success out in the future. Your calling is your faithfulness to God *today*.

You aren't called to a work. You're called to a transformation. Because truth be told, *he's* the one doing the work anyway! Yes, your life is about populating heaven. Your purpose is to represent him. But the good news is, God doesn't need your abilities but your *availability*. He doesn't need you to be prepared already. He just needs you to be usable. Because if you make your priority to know him every day, opportunities in your life will arise where you will have a chance to share Jesus. And the good news is, from then on, you're completely out of control; he is doing all the work through you.

See, we get this all confused. We base spiritual success off an outcome of *our* work. We think God is pleased with us *only* when we do something for him first. But God never asked anything from you. He has always just wanted your heart. And the more you seek him, the more you will allow the Spirit to come in and work through you to other people.

So how do you know? If you aren't constantly searching for people to impact, how will you know whether to step in and do something or not? This is where *abiding* is so important. The closer you walk to the Spirit and the closer you get to know him, the better you will hear him. He will direct you, nudge you, compel you to do all sorts of things in his name. And if something is placed on your heart, act on it! Remember, you're in charge of obedience, not outcome. So if the Lord has placed something on your heart for you to do, you choosing to obey and follow through is the only thing he's asking for. He takes the whole saving part out of your hands.

I firmly believe God gives each of us spiritual gifts. Scripture even says it; everyone has been given a unique set of things they are good at to help reflect God and his glory (1 Corinthians 12:4–11, Romans 12:5–8). Recall our verse at the beginning of this section. God has created good works for *you* in Christ Jesus before you were even born, and with this comes something I like to call a *divine burden*. Today, there is *something* on your heart that stirs and causes a spiritual uproar inside you. Something just doesn't sit right. It could be people who aren't loved, people in need, people without hope, joy, or peace, people who were overlooked, people who were left for nothing, people who need encouragement. There is *something* that was divinely placed on your heart that causes you to hurt. And once you identify that, you can identify where God has called you to be.

Remember, you can't save the whole world. In fact, *you* can't even save one person! Christ is the one in charge of that. But you *can* be available and obey. Scripture says we are living temples of the Spirit living inside us (1 Corinthians 6:19). And since Christ has given us the Spirit to help us do his work, we no longer have to work alone.

Calling is not a success in the future. Calling is your faithfulness and obedience today. God never asked for your abilities. He just needs your *availability.*

Lord, I am open and available to anything and everything you place on my heart.

"But you shall receive power when the Holy Spirit has come upon you; and you shall be witnesses to Me in Jerusalem, and in all Judea and Samaria, and to the end of the earth" (Acts 1:8).

Getting It Right

This chapter has touched specifically on following Jesus and identifying exactly what he did and how he lived. In order to *know* and follow him, it's important we look at how he did things. And to close, I want to look at something we as Christians actually get *wrong.*

"And the Word became flesh and dwelt among us, and we beheld His glory, the glory as of the only begotten of the Father, full of grace and truth" (John 1:14).

And the Word became flesh and dwelt among us. And he was full of what? Grace and truth.

Sometimes, we get that wrong.

The truth is, we are called to live and love with grace and truth. But the problem is, if you look at the world we live in today, we are so far from it. Especially as people who claim to be followers of Christ, someone who came with both, we find ourselves on opposite sides of the spectrum. If a fellow faithful believer stumbles in a moment of temptation? Truth. *You're a sinner. God could never love you. You're going to hell!* But if someone who loves to sin falls short of the glory of God—grace. *It's okay. God doesn't care about how you live. Jesus has already forgiven you anyway. Don't worry about it.*

How do we get it wrong? Because instead of coming with both grace and truth, we come with only one, if any. But that simply cannot happen. And today, we're going to declare change. We're going to get it right, not to be on an opposite side of the spectrum but right in the middle, just like Jesus was.

This is the common problem—we either have no grace and complete truth, or we have no truth and abuse grace. These two extremes create two extremely big problems. And this is what ends up happening:

1. *Truth without grace leads to rebellion.*

    If all we do is pound people with truth after truth after truth, eventually, we as humans decide to give up. "You have to live this way. You have to follow this rule. You have to act like this." And after countless tries of truth, truth, truth, people just rebel. *Who are they to tell me what to do? Why should I let them tell me how to live? Their expectations are way too high for me, so I'm just going to do it my own way.*

    If we deal with people with no empathy, no love, no grace, people will reject what you say and will rebel hard against it. I mean, think about it. If you have an extremely religious and legalistic home, what do you almost always see from the children? Rebellion. Because when you lead with rules and religion without relationship, people do not invest themselves into it. Leading with truth almost guarantees a perception of God as a demanding judge, not a loving Father.

2. *Grace without truth leads to relativism.*

On the other hand, if all you live with is grace, you are creating a misconception of what grace actually is. Remember, grace is not an obligation to sin—it's a freedom not to. And if all you lead with is grace, grace, grace, people will get the conception that you can do whatever the heck you want without any kind of standard.

Grace without truth leads people to the conclusion that it doesn't matter what you do, as long as you're happy. It doesn't really matter what you believe, as long as you're sincere. It doesn't really matter how you live unless you don't hurt anybody. Because without truth, there is acceptance without any type of definitive measure.

So, how do we respond? How do we fix this problem of one side or the other and come to a median of responding with both?

Big point: grace saves, but truth frees.

1. *Grace saves.*

"For by grace you have been saved through faith, and that not of yourselves; it is the gift of God, not of works, lest anyone should boast" (Ephesians 2:8–9).

It is by *grace* that you have been saved. Nowhere in Scripture will you find that truth is the only way to salvation. We must remember, first and foremost, that grace is the leading factor to repentance. A changed heart will never find genuine repentance if the leading factor is truth. Jesus said the greatest commandment was to love God and then your neighbor as yourself (Matthew 22:37–39). *That* is grace—replicating the love, the forgiveness, the mercy, and the grace of your Savior.

Look at John 1:14 again. What did Jesus come full of? Grace and truth. Which one comes first?

Grace.

Because truth is not what saves you. Grace is. And grace is always the most important factor when reflecting Jesus.

2. *Truth frees.*

Although truth cannot save you, truth can *free* you. John 8:32 says, "And you shall know the truth, and the truth shall make you free." Truth is what frees you from this life of sin and death. And the truth is, Jesus is inviting you into a new life away from sin, shame, unholiness, and bondage. You *can* be set free by the truth.

When dealing with people, it's important to remember that grace saves, but truth frees. Yes, you are forgiven. Grace is calling your name. But the truth of the matter is, Jesus has a *better life* in store for you, away from the passing desires of this world. There is freedom in knowing him and in obedience. And the good news is, his grace will always be enough when you fall.

Who needs grace? Does the rebellious teen need grace? What about the perfect daughter who wouldn't hurt a soul? Or your friend that has turned their back on you? Or your family member who has treated you unfairly or incorrectly?

Or you?

Who needs grace?

The answer? Everyone. *We* need grace. Thank God Jesus didn't come just full of truth. Because it is by grace you have been saved! You are no longer a slave to your sin or a captive to the grave. You are freely forgiven. His grace is unmerited and undeserved. But he gives it away time after time after time.

"But God demonstrates His own love toward us, in that while we were still sinners, Christ died for us" (Romans 5:8).

The truth of the matter is—we have fallen short. We *do not* deserve God's love. That is the coldhearted truth.

But *in* God's grace, he sent Jesus. And while we were yet sinners, he died in our place. And if Christ can lead and love with grace and truth, so should we.

"If you keep My commandments, you will abide in My love, just as I have kept My Father's commandments and abide in His love" (John 15:10).

CHAPTER 6

Eternity Awaits

Citizen of Heaven

If you look through any of the gospels, you'll be able to quickly identify what Jesus spoke about most: the kingdom of God. In everything he said, there was always a parallel and relation back to heaven and eternity. All his actions, his choices, his words, his decisions—they all point toward eternity.

> Therefore let that abide in you which you heard from the beginning. If what you heard from the beginning abides in you, you also will abide in the Son and in the Father. And this is the promise that He has promised us—eternal life. (1 John 2:24–25)

Why does this matter? Because if Jesus prioritized living with an eternal perspective, we should too. Philippians 3:20 says, "For our citizenship is in heaven, from which we also eagerly wait for the Savior, the Lord Jesus Christ." See, most of us have chosen heaven over hell. We have accepted Christ as Lord and have eternally secured our life beyond the grave by grace alone. But the problem is, some of us have trouble choosing heaven over *earth*. Although we know, someday, we'll be a citizen of heaven, we don't live like one today.

Everything you do in this life is preparing you for the next one. First John 3:2–3 says:

> Beloved, now we are children of God; and it has not yet been revealed what we shall be, but we know that when He is revealed, we shall be like Him, for we shall see Him as He is. And everyone who has this hope in Him purifies himself, just as He is pure.

If we live every day, eagerly expecting his return, we naturally will have a longing, desire to honor him with our lives. Notice the cause and effect here. The more you think about eternity and his return, the more you will desire keeping his commandments.

Now, don't confuse this. Waiting for his return and living pure *will not* earn God's favor. You choosing to live a certain way and maintaining a certain mindset will not dictate his love for you. However, we've decided we want to do everything short of sin we can to get closer to Jesus. And if you *deeply* desire to know him, you must know his will. Jesus prioritized eternity. And living with this eternal perspective in mind will draw you closer and closer to him and his goodness.

The way you view life beyond the grave will have complete influence on how you choose to live your life today. If you believe there is no life beyond the grave, chances are you'll live recklessly. You won't care for people. You won't see a need to live holy. You'll find no purpose for God. And you'll see no need for humility. If you don't believe there's life beyond the grave, chances are, you will live a selfish, personal, self-centered, all-or-nothing type of life with no meaning or purpose beyond *now.*

YOLO.

Maybe you do believe there's eternity. You do believe there's life beyond the grave. But the problem is, you only believe in heaven. Hell? Not a thing. God surely won't send anyone to hell. He knows your heart. You're a good person. *You'll be fine.* Live however you want because, in the end, it won't really matter. *You do, you boo.*

The greatest lie Satan can ever make you believe is that eternity isn't a big deal. If he can somehow make you think that heaven isn't home and eternity isn't important, you're lost. Because eternity is the basis of all God's creation. God intended for man to live with him *forever* in his presence. And if you forget that point, you are storing up all your treasures in a world that does not last. If you really think about it, so often, we find ourselves torn between believing what Jesus says. We love to hear about heaven. But any thought of hell is almost banished nowadays in the church.

Here's the catch: Jesus spoke on both.

Eternal living has to be the center point. Paul spoke about this in 1 Corinthians 15. He says in verses 17–19:

> And if Christ is not risen, your faith is futile; you are still in your sins! Then also those who have fallen asleep in Christ have perished. If in this life only we have hope in Christ, we are of all men the most pitiable.

Paul makes this crystal clear. If your faith in Jesus is *not* centered around eternity, you are more to be pitied than anyone else! Why? Because heaven is the center of everything that Jesus came for. If you follow Jesus in hopes of personal gain and benefit for this life only, your faith is useless. Useless! Because if Jesus didn't save you from your sins eternally, there is no other reason to follow him. Your relationship with Christ will never be based upon the gifts he brings or the blessings he gives. It will always come back to the way God designed for you and me to find everlasting life and rest beyond the grave.

Why does this matter? Because if you put eternity at the forefront of your faith, then the way you view God, the way you live, and the perspective you have will drastically change. Everything you do will have a reason behind it, centered upon eternity. All the things you experience will relate back to how you view eternity. And everything you *go* through can be overcome based upon the peace eternity can bring. It all comes back in the end.

You weren't put on earth to be remembered. You were put here to prepare for eternal life.

This chapter is the most important chapter in this book. I say this with extreme caution because a lot of this can very easily be taken out of context. I pray that the Lord will speak to you in a certain way specific for your heart and ask that he reveals something to you that will change your faith forever. I *truly* believe having an eternal perspective through life is the way to breakthrough, perfect peace, and freedom. As we walk through this concept, keep your heart open and ask the Spirit to guide you in your thinking. Because, in the end, *everything* you do is preparing you to experience Jesus forever in eternity. And we should be thinking about that continually.

The Thing I Seek Most—

What matters most to you?

Over the course of your life, this question is the most important question you will ever wrestle with. Out of your entire existence, in this life and the next, what *single* thing do you cherish most?

What does your heart long for?

There are so many options. You could desire fame, money, power, possessions, the list goes on. You also could desire success, appreciation, acceptance, or recognition. Or maybe you're not as materialistic; maybe you truly desire contentment, peace, joy, or happiness. But the fact of the matter is, as you identify what matters most to you in your life, you must realize that *everything* you do reflects that value. How you live, how you treat others, what your motives are—everything is centered upon your deepest and longest desire.

Take a moment and really think about it. You don't have to just read over these words and make up some random answer. Be honest. Be vulnerable. Reflect today on the core values of your heart. This isn't designed to make you feel guilty; this is designed to assist you in highlighting where and what your motives are formed from. In all your entire existence, from here on into eternity, what is the number one thing you wish to receive, attain, or experience?

What matters most to you?

In order to experience a true, intimate relationship with Jesus, we have to prioritize what's to come. Now, I use the words *have to* very lightly. Again, living with an eternal perspective will not change the way God sees you. You are saved by grace, not works, and made right with God by faith, not by the law (Ephesians 2:8–9, Galatians 2:16). So really, the word that should be used is *can*. You *can* experience a deeper and intimate relationship with Jesus when you put eternity at the forefront. That's true gospel language—always your free choice.

Look what King David says in Psalm 27: "One thing I have desired of the Lord, that will I seek:

That I may dwell in the house of the Lord all the days of my life, to behold the beauty of the Lord, and to inquire in His temple" (v. 4). What is the *one* thing David sought after? What mattered most to him? To be in his presence. The most important thing to David, out of his entire existence, was to dwell in the house of the Lord. That's it. He wasn't focused on defeating enemies or conquering land or being the best king of Israel, none of that. Scripture says he was a "man after God's own heart" (1 Samuel 13:14). David cared the most about experiencing the Lord and his presence in a deep, intimate way. And *everything* he did was influenced by this one desire.

What mattered most to King David? His intimacy with God.

This sounds like such an easy answer, but if you look at the way we live, sometimes, we can say the complete opposite. Do you *truly* value your relationship with God as most important? Again, this isn't a guilt trip question to answer. This is a breakthrough opportunity that is identifying where you put your utmost interests. If you, today, *truly* desire to know Jesus in a close and intimate way—you can. But it all starts with the center motive of the heart.

The reason why we don't prioritize heaven is because we have an obscured view of what heaven actually is like. Heaven is not some default destination where we go when we die. Heaven is home! Recall what Paul said in Philippians 1:21, "For to me, to live is Christ, and to die is gain." Paul says dying is *better* for him because, then, he will be in his most glorious state—present with the Lord. See, death isn't the end of some glorious run; death is the beginning of brand-new life. Heaven isn't a cage we get locked into beyond the grave. Heaven is where we finally get our chains *removed.*

Here are three very common misconceptions about heaven:

Heaven will be boring.

This is the most common misconception of what heaven is. *It's boring! There's nothing to do there. It's nowhere close to being as fun as earth. Man, when I get to heaven, there's going to be a lot of sitting around and playing the harp.* All these accusations are not true and almost incompetent to what heaven is really like.

> Eye has not seen, nor ear heard, nor have entered into the heart of man the things which God has prepared for those who love Him. (1 Corinthians 2:9)

> Let not your heart be troubled; you believe in God, believe also in Me. In My Father's house are many mansions; if it were not so, I would have told you. I go to prepare a place for you. And if I go and prepare a place for you, I will come again and receive you to Myself; that where I am, there you may be also. And where I go you know, and the way you know. (John 14:1–4)

> And I heard a loud voice from heaven saying, "Behold, the tabernacle of God is with men, and He will dwell with them, and they shall be His people. God Himself will be with them and be their God." (Revelation 21:3)

Heaven is not a blank space. Heaven is the literal reality of being in the presence of God. And in the presence of God, there will be perfection—no more sin, no more shame, no more pain, no more tears. There will be *no* more sorrow and no more disappointment. Everything will be renewed. There will be healing, restoration, redemption, revival, community, purity, honor, and so much more. Heaven is good. And in the midst of the Lord's presence, you will no longer be surrounded by a sinful world but overtaken by a sinless God. We will know one another, love, and be loved (1 Corinthians 13:12–13). You will see Jesus face-to-face (1 John 3:2). Ultimately, heaven is the absence of everything bad, painful, and evil and the presence of everything good, holy, and glorious (Isaiah 65:17–25). There will be no faults. Amid God's presence and goodness, you will be entered into a brand-new reality full of love, community, and wholeness.

"And God will wipe away every tear from their eyes; there shall be no more death, nor sorrow, nor crying. There shall be no more pain, for the former things have passed away" (Revelation 21:4).

Heaven is not home.

The fact of the matter is this—many Christians do not treat heaven as home. We treat earth as home, and the thought of death could be compared to a going-away trip. Heaven is just somewhere we go and visit—but this isn't the case. Heaven is not a luck of the draw reality you end up at, where things get worse from how they were before. It's home. Heaven is where you belong. And if you are treating heaven like vacation more than home, you are forgetting the glories of ultimate eternity.

Sometimes, we all fall into this trap. We live our lives here on earth completely forgetting about the length and meaning of heaven. We fall victim to allowing Satan to make us think we belong here and will always stay here, but that's just simply not the case. Jesus did not forgive your sins so that you could be forgiven physically. He didn't die on the cross for you to live your life on earth proclaiming you are forgiven. He died for your *spiritual* state. Your sins are forgiven eternally; meaning, you have been granted life beyond the grave. So if eternity is the focus, why aren't we living like it?

> While we do not look at the things which are seen, but at the things which are not seen. For the things which are seen are temporary, but the things which are not seen are eternal. (2 Corinthians 4:18)

> If then you were raised with Christ, seek those things which are above, where Christ is, sitting at the right hand of God. Set your mind on things above, not on things on the earth. For you died, and your life is hidden with Christ in God. When Christ who is our life appears, then you also will appear with Him in glory. (Colossians 3:1–4)

The life you live is only a mist—a vapor, a speck of dust compared to eternity. You have to remember—absent from the body, present with the Lord. This world is not your home. Heaven is. And the more you look to heaven for revival and hope, the more you will find yourself longing to be in the presence of God.

Earth is temporary. Heaven is eternal.

Most people are going to heaven anyway.

All around the world today, so many people wrongly believe that most people are going to heaven anyway.

There's no reason to live for heaven because we are all going to end up there regardless. Don't waste your time. You only live once! Experience as much as you can. Feel it. Do it. Describe it. Take it in. Live the way you want. Because ultimately, it doesn't matter—everyone is going to heaven. I'm good enough. I don't do the really bad things. I'm going to heaven anyway—so it doesn't matter how I live today.

> Not everyone who says to Me, "Lord,
> Lord," shall enter the kingdom of heaven, but he
> who does the will of My Father in heaven. Many
> will say to Me in that day, "Lord, Lord, have we
> not prophesied in Your name, cast out demons
> in Your name, and done many wonders in Your
> name?" And then I will declare to them, "I never
> knew you; depart from Me, you who practice
> lawlessness!" (Matthew 7:21–23)

How come we act like we deserve heaven?

How do we just magically think we deserve to live forever after we die? Are we perfect? Are we sinless? Scripture is pretty clear—all have sinned and fallen short of the glory of God (Romans 3:23).

The truth of the matter is this: good people don't go to heaven when they die. *Forgiven* people go to heaven when they die.

Forgiven by the grace of Jesus, justified by the righteousness of God, brought to new life through the resurrection of the Son—*that's* how you get to heaven. Not by good works, not by selfless deeds, not by perfect behavior but through Jesus Christ our Lord.

> Jesus said to her, "I am the resurrection and
> the life. The one who believes in me will live, even
> though they die; and whoever lives by believing
> in me will never die. Do you believe this?" (John
> 11:25–26)

I want you to internalize this. I want this to hit you deeply in a way it never did before. It was not by your goodness or earned behavior but in God's grace that he sent his Son. We don't deserve it; none of us do. But in God's rich mercy, he sent Jesus to climb the mountain we could never climb.

This is why we sing. This is why we are so passionate about the goodness of the gospel. Because without Jesus, I am a lost soul, I am doomed for eternity, and I am on course for hell. My sins have separated me, and my evil has corrupted me. I'm simply not good enough. I could never be. There is no way for myself, in my own power, to meet God's glorious standard of perfection and righteousness.

But in his loving kindness, God said I don't have to be good enough because Jesus already is. Jesus is good enough. And when he took my place on that cross and I accepted his free gift of grace, I was forever good enough in his eyes, not because of anything I've done but because of everything he has done.

Oh, how I long to breathe the air of heaven. That is my most important priority in everything I do—to walk with him for all eternity.

Holy, holy is the Lord.

Keeping an Eternal Perspective

If God originally intended for us to live forever, we can conclude that when we get to heaven, only then will we become everything he has created us to be. And this is good news, knowing that although we follow Jesus daily in hopes of replicating him, God still does not expect perfection. Following Jesus is not a works-based faith. Following Jesus is an intention of the inner heart to know and honor him with all your life. And if you really know Jesus and God's love for you, you will have a longing desire to be as perfect as you can be. That doesn't mean you will be—but it does mean you will try.

This is a process theologically referred to as sanctification, and over the next section, we are going to get into how the daily life of a Christ believer is one step closer toward righteousness. Again, this is a very deep topic and can very easily be misunderstood. So as you read, open up your heart and ask God to speak to you in a way that is (1) gospel-based and (2) Scripture-supported. Not only does talking about eternity affect how we live today but what we believe happens there also has the utmost effect.

There are two words that can explain the current processes for a Christian—justification and sanctification. These words are vital to understanding eternity because both play a huge role in your journey to righteousness. Justification is through Jesus Christ alone (Acts

4:12), and there is nothing you can do to earn your way to heaven. The only way you can enter is through the blood of the lamb, accepting the grace he reflected on the cross and recognizing him as Lord and Savior. Salvation comes from nothing except the Son of God, and heaven itself is only available through knowing Jesus.

However, the other word, *sanctification*, is up to the believer. Sanctification is the daily, ongoing process of becoming more and more like Christ. It is the never-ending road of pursuing and seeking that brings you closer to who Jesus is and how he lived. In other words, sanctification is how you live. You can look at it as *justification* is your identity (in Christ), and *sanctification* is your character (becoming like Christ). We enter the kingdom because of our new birth and because we have received God's Spirit. But we inherit the kingdom as a reward for an obedient and faithful lifestyle here on earth. Everything you do now is a preparation to experience Jesus in an intimate way in eternity. Now, do not mistake it—we will never do it perfectly. We will never, in this life, be able to perform sinless and complete righteous living. But we will recognize our choices and continue to choose to follow Christ the best we can.

If, at this point, you are thinking to yourself questions like— is this me? Am I good enough? Will God call me faithful? Let me remind you—sanctification is not earned because of perfection. Sanctification happens because of intention, faithfulness, perseverance. Righteousness is a sign of intent and purpose behind one's life, one's decisions, and one's faithfulness. God is not looking for perfect performance or behavior. He is looking for a faithful, Christ-seeking individual whose number one intention is to live their life for him. That's it. You see a behavior change because of your eagerness out of love, not your perfection out of fear.

Being conformed into his image is critically important. Being a living example of Christ is what will bring others to the Lord, and Scripture describes his second coming when God promised David a Messiah would come from his bloodline and remain on the throne (2 Samuel 7:12–13). He will have a thousand-year period of rule on earth as king, just as God promised from the beginning. And with the way we choose to live now, when that time comes, you will either be alongside him in glory or still needing to develop your faithfulness in due time. It's a matter of when you are choosing to get ready: now or eternity? Because our life here on earth is simply the training ground, the proving ground, and the testing ground for the next life.

Thankfully, God doesn't expect us to become perfect in this life. Scripture also describes how we will receive "resurrected bodies" when he comes again (1 Thessalonians 4:16–17, Romans 8:23–26, 1 Corinthians 15:40–50). This is clear that we are not expected to be perfect now because our sinful bodies won't allow it. But it does promise that we will experience complete transformation when we pass over from this life to the next.

If you are currently reading this message and a wave of fear and doubt has crept into your mind about your own life, know that it's not too late. You are not too far, and you can turn around today. If, deep down, you know that your motives are not pointed toward God and your life does not really reflect a deep relationship with him full of love, make the move today. Sanctification is not earned by lengthy periods of having a perfect relationship with him. Sanctification happens because of a true repentance and wanting a change of heart. It is a deeply devoted will to truly know Jesus intimately and really honor God with your life. It's no longer a look from the outside in, only using God when you need him. It's committing your entire life to him, as a living sacrifice, and allowing his Spirit to change you from the inside out. Again, he doesn't need perfect behavior. He just needs you to come. Because once you do come as you are, he will do the work in you that you need.

If you value intimacy with Jesus, sanctification will be your first and foremost priority in life, not because you have to but because you want to have this deep, meaningful relationship with your creator. Thinking about eternity is not designed to make people feel like they have to follow Jesus. It's simply a confirmation from God that he sees your faithfulness and desire to know him. Heaven is waiting for your arrival, and if, today, you feel like what you are doing doesn't matter and you aren't getting anywhere, you can trust in this truth:

God *will* reward you for your faithfulness and perseverance. And when the time does come, you will hear those awe-striking words: "Well done, my good and faithful servant" (Matthew 25:21).

Keep fighting the good fight. We're almost home.

Jesus Is True Life

Now, let's throw all of this together.

Having an eternal perspective changes everything. True, lasting joy is found only in living *for* heaven, where the glitter and highs of this world have lost its glamour and power. Living with an eternal perspective is not just denying reality and ignoring everything we have on earth. Living with an eternal perspective is a faith statement that deliberately chooses Jesus and his kingdom as a full satisfaction source. You're not living out of touch with this world; rather, you are in touch with Christ as your life source *for* this world.

He is inviting you into a better life full of freedom, peace, and joy.

"Jesus spoke to the people once more and said, 'I am the light of the world. If you follow me, you won't have to walk in darkness, because you will have the light that leads to life'" (John 8:12 NLT).

Notice what Jesus is saying here. He *is* the light of the world. He *is* a life-giving source. He *is* the way to the Father! And if you so choose to follow him, you *won't have* to walk in darkness! Stop for a minute and embrace these gospel-based words. Jesus did not say you *aren't allowed to.* He isn't forcing you to honor some religious practice. He says you *won't have to.* There's a better way! And when you find him, he promises you will have the light that leads to life.

In my very short time here on earth, I've chased after so many things. I sought satisfaction and happiness in materials, people, success, accolades, only to be left empty and broken time and time again. I was stuck in this cycle of *trying* to *earn* contentment and working for what I wanted, which, in the end, never even provided.

I chased after materials, thinking clothing or objects could bring me joy. I got my feet wet in relationships, going from person to person, hoping they would make me feel a little more appreciated. I thought maybe, just maybe, if I became the best athlete there ever was, I would finally be at peace within myself. I tried fame and popularity, hoping that the more people knew who I was, the more I would get recognized for my worth.

But in the end—they all failed. Every single one of them. Because a sinful world can never offer you abundant fulfillment. It's impossible. And as I was looking for true life outside the life himself, I felt more and more of a conviction to come running back to him.

And he picked me up, just like he always does.

Remember what we said earlier: *true* life begins only when Jesus becomes the source of it. If you really want to experience abundant life, full to the top with joy, peace, and love, you will only find it in Jesus because he is the *same* for all our days and his faithfulness never changes.

You don't have to take on this world alone. You have the *same* Spirit power in you that rose Christ from the dead (Romans 8:11). You can overcome, choosing to keep an eternal perspective through every trial and even every triumph. There is a promise in Scripture that if you cling to Christ, he will carry you through the rest of your life and into eternity (Hebrews 13:5). Don't wait another minute! Embrace this new, abundant life Jesus is inviting you to.

> We are hard-pressed on every side, yet not crushed; we are perplexed, but not in despair; persecuted, but not forsaken; struck down, but not destroyed—always carrying about in the body the dying of the Lord Jesus, that the life of Jesus also may be manifested in our body. For we who live are always delivered to death for Jesus' sake, that the life of Jesus also may be manifested in our mortal flesh. So then death is working in us, but life in you. (2 Corinthians 4:8–12)

> Therefore we do not lose heart. Even though our outward man is perishing, yet the inward man is being renewed day by day. For our light

affliction, which is but for a moment, is working
for us a far more exceeding and eternal weight of
glory, while we do not look at the things which
are seen, but at the things which are not seen.
For the things which are seen are temporary,
but the things which are not seen are eternal. (2
Corinthians 4:16–18)

Sure, we'll face hardship here. We'll run into trouble. But we
will *not* be crushed. We might get knocked down, but we will *not* be
destroyed. We *will not* give up! Because even though we have troubles, they are producing a glory inside us that will last forever. What
we see now? It'll soon be gone. Instead, we choose to fix our gaze on
the unseen—what will last forever.

This is the true meaning of abundant life. Remember the Greek
word for abundant, *perissos*, which means "far greater, excessive, or
exceeding than what you can think of." If there is truly a far greater
and excessive life somewhere, we can trust in the promise that it can
be found in Christ alone. Following Jesus isn't just something you
do occasionally. Following Jesus is the source of which you live. He
isn't an add-on but, rather, your *entire* source of life that gives you
meaning and purpose. He isn't *forcing* you. He is *inviting* you into a
relational, intimate love that will carry you into eternity.

Why not take it?

CONCLUSION

Eternal Living Starts Now

Woohoo. We finally made it.

Over the course of this book, we've talked solely about one big point: intimately knowing Jesus. It has been my goal to lead and show you how and what to do in order to really know Jesus deeply. And after this long road, I pray that if you take anything from this book, you remember our key word: *abide.*

Remember what I said at the beginning of the book? The moment I read through the entire Bible, front to back, was the moment I *finally* had my chains broken. I finally recognized what God desired from his people and finally understood the true power of grace. Reading the Bible from cover to cover radically transformed my life.

So we're going to go through it.

What? Don't worry, we aren't reading through the *entire* Bible. We're going to go over the major events, prophecies, promises, and happenings that went on throughout Scripture. If we are Christians, we believe the Bible. And if we truly honor the Word of God, everything it says is true. Now, do not get this confused—just because you read this conclusion doesn't mean you have read through the entire Bible and can check that off your list of spiritual disciplines. This is just an overview of what exactly it conveys and an opportunity for general understanding of what it says about everything. This won't give you *every* detail you'd like to know, but it will highlight key aspects when dealing with understanding Scripture. Don't be overwhelmed. Ask the Spirit to guide you as you read how everything came into fruition.

Understanding the Bible changes everything. But before we start, I want you to keep one word in the back of your mind. As you read each section, Old *and* New Testament, I want this word to be your main focus for everything you understand: *redemption*.

Okay. Let's do this.

In the beginning, God created the heavens and the earth (Genesis 1:1). In the beginning, God. He's *always* been there. He was perfect already; by himself, he needed no addition. But out of his great love, he created the heavens and the earth.

Then, Genesis 1:26 tells us that God made man: "Let us make human beings in Our image, according to Our likeness." God, because he *cherished* us, created mankind in his *own image*. That is super exciting news! We were created in the image of God, carrying his love and approval with us wherever we go. We are children of the Most High. And when God created Adam and Eve, his desire was to walk with them in the garden of Eden, loving and protecting them through whatever they did or wherever they went.

But something happened. Something *wrong* happened. God told Adam and Eve that they could not eat from the tree of the knowledge of good and evil (Genesis 2:16). Out of every tree in the garden, the only one they couldn't touch was this one. But as Satan, appearing as a serpent, came, seeking to disrupt this fellowship with God and man, Adam and Eve were tempted to do something they knew they shouldn't do. And after justifying their decision, *both* man and woman ate from this tree, resulting in the first ever sin by mankind.

Adam and Eve turned against God. They were in the wrong. They used something from God's good creation and misused its purpose entirely. And as soon as they sinned, they felt a wave of guilt and shame, hiding from God in the garden (Genesis 3:10). We do the same thing today. In our sin, instead of running toward God for forgiveness, we run away from God in shame, and that's exactly how they both felt. God is love, but God is also just; every time sin enters the equation, something must be inflicted to pay the punishment for it. And because of that first sin, now, the entire world from here on out would be cursed with the same sense of evil.

Boom. That was it. That was all Satan needed to corrupt the world we live in. And to this very day, because of that first slip up, we live in a broken, sinful world. But God didn't quit; he didn't want to leave man in the broken state we were in. So God continued to watch over his created people, leading generation to generation with love. And eventually, we find a man named Abram (God later changed his name to Abraham), who was *extremely* faithful to God. And because he was so faithful, God made a promise to him that he would bless him with numerous descendants and watch over them for generations to come (Genesis 12:1–3). God made a promise not to leave or forsake Abraham. And eventually, he gave birth to two sons (Ishmael and Isaac). Then, through Isaac, we have Jacob and Esau, which, through Jacob, comes Joseph, one of his twelve sons.

Long story short, after Joseph's lifetime, a new Pharaoh rose and enslaved all the Israelites (Exodus 1:8–11). So now, God's people were in bondage. They were taken captive by the Egyptians and were forced into labor. Quite a turn of events, considering they were supposed to be blessed.

But there was a reason. They weren't perfect. Generations had come and gone that indulged in sin. And because they were enslaved, they were forced into bondage and oppression. But God, in his great love again, called up Moses to lead these people out of Egypt. Now, understand that Moses wasn't the most qualified guy. He was afraid, insecure, and he even had a speech problem (Exodus 4:10). But the reality was, Moses wasn't called because he was prepared. He was called because God *chose* him. He wasn't the best of the best in any way. He simply was a chosen instrument used by God for big, kingdom purposes—just like you.

So Moses went. Led by God (Exodus 4:15), Moses led the enslaved people out of bondage. They were free. And God directed them in the way they should go to eventually reach a place he had prepared for them all along: the Promised Land. He parted the Red Sea, provided food for them, even helped them attack any possible enemies they faced. The Lord was with them—not because they deserved his help but because he loved them enough to save them.

On their long journey to this treasured land, God gave Moses a set of rules for the people to follow. Up on Mount Sanai, he gave them the covenant and the law to instruct them on how to live. God didn't give them the law to simply condemn them; he gave it to *expose* their sinful nature. They needed to be aware. And along with this covenant, the people created a tabernacle for the Spirit of the Lord to dwell in. Everywhere they went, they carried this ark with them that held the presence of the Lord. This is really important for later understanding.

With this covenant was a way to redeem sin. If the people ever sinned, they could sacrifice an animal as an offering to be made right again with God. So every time they sinned, they were required, by law, to repay the debt with a life of an animal. This is also really important for later understanding.

But after all of this, the people still had issues. They complained about their circumstance, not believing God would make a way. They blamed God for not providing them with enough food. They even went as far as saying they wanted to go *back* to Egypt into slavery because it would be better for them!

Don't we do the same thing?

Just like Peter from earlier, when we feel abandoned or don't see a way out, we go back to what's comfortable. We go back into hostage to our fears, worries, and doubts. For crying out loud, the Israelites wanted to be *enslaved* again, simply because they didn't trust God to lead them! But God stayed faithful. He didn't leave them, and eventually, they made it to the Promised Land, a promise he made to Abraham all the way back in Genesis 15:15–21.

After all the wandering and all the complaining, God brought them to this treasured area. This was now called Israel. They were *given* this land solely because God loved them. But even with all these blessings, the Israelites *still* didn't trust him and asked for a physical king to rule. They didn't think God was enough to plan and protect them from the world around them. So apart from his intended will, he allowed a man named Saul to become king, which ended up not working. And after all the confusion and conflict, God finally arose his chosen king from the start: a little boy named David. David was an unlikely hero. He was the youngest son of Jesse and was always overlooked by everyone around him. But it didn't matter what people thought because God *already* chose him, just like God has *already* chosen you.

Fast-forward a bit. David became king. He attempted to lead the people. But the Israelites completely ran from God. The nations raged, and Israel fell into serious idolatry, turning their backs on the God who carried them all along. They broke the covenant, they left God in the dust, and they prioritized sin. And because God is just, sin *must* be punished, except the punishment this time around was something the people knew far too well: captivity.

The Israelites were bound to be enslaved again, this time by the Babylonians. But God sent prophets to speak in his name and warn the people about the coming judgment. The only problem was, they didn't listen and, quite frankly, they didn't even care. They carried on in their sin, running even further from God than before, and lined themselves up perfectly for another captivity. Now, these prophets weren't special either; they were chosen by God to notify the people about (1) Israel's soon downfall and (2) a coming Messiah for redemption. God told them to endure the storm ahead, knowing he *will* stay faithful and keep his promise to save. So in the end, the people were taken captive by the Babylonian empire.

For seventy years, they were held in captivity. *Seventy years.* And in the middle of that, they questioned God. They abandoned God. They blamed God. They cried out to him for help. They were stuck in this never-ending cycle of ignoring the elephant in the room: their sin. They wanted so badly just to be set free and have comfortability again that they forget they sinned against a holy and sovereign God. And after all their idolatry, they finally had to pay for it.

Fast-forward again. Eventually, Babylon got conquered, and the Israelites were allowed to return home to rebuild their land. They prioritized rebuilding the Temple and the wall surrounding the city, but when they got there, they completely forgot about it. They spent their time building their own towers before the wall (Haggai 1:3–5).

They also almost quit building the Temple because they didn't think it would look as good as the previous one. And on top of that, they faced extreme opposition by other people when rebuilding the temple of the Lord (Nehemiah 4:1–2). But they carried on, thinking how they could make it up to God. They had ideas, such as thousands of burnt offerings or lengthy periods of perfect behavior, but in the end, it never worked.

And the Old Testament came to an end.

But then, God is silent. Like *completely* silent. Known as the intertestamental period, God was completely silent toward his people for four hundred years. Four hundred years! Not a word, not a glimpse of hope. There was no voice from God. The only thing that gave them hope was the promise of a Messiah.

All throughout the Old Testament, we see prophecies of Jesus's coming. God *promised* King David that his house will forever reign on the throne (2 Samuel 7:12–16). This promise is known as the Davidic Covenant—that there will always be someone from David's line of descendants to rule and reign. And from what we see in Matthew 1:16, Jesus is the messianic king, who came all the way from the line of David.

See, God planned it all along. He divinely ordered existence and time to bring Jesus in the mix right when he was supposed to. But that's not all. All throughout the Old Testament, prophecies containing the birth of Christ were given to be later fulfilled: the place of his birth (Micah 5:2), which was Bethlehem (later fulfilled in Matthew 2:5–6); the manner of his birth (Isaiah 7:14), which was a virgin birth from Mary (later fulfilled in Matthew 1:22–23).

To make it even cooler than it already was, God prophesied all the way back in Genesis that the scepter will come from Judah:

"The scepter shall not depart from Judah, nor a lawgiver from between his feet, until Shiloh comes; and to Him shall be the obedience of the people" (Genesis 49:10).

Jesus wasn't just a last-minute idea. Jesus was divinely planned all along. And the king of glory came like a baby in the manger, born in a stable in Bethlehem. The Son of God was born (prophesied in

Isaiah 9:6). And after a conversation with the angel Gabriel, Mary and Joseph knew that Jesus was the coming king.

Jesus lived a sinless life. He was completely perfect, being the standard and leader of everything God created man to be. Jesus was a *divine being*, who became *flesh* just for you and me! Jesus loved everybody throughout his lifetime. He healed, forgave, encouraged, redeemed, revived, and restored. He was the way to God all along (John 14:6), and everyone missed out on that, so much so that he was destined for a death by crucifixion on a cross.

Jesus understood his mission though. He came to die (John 3:17). He told all the disciples about it and how he would rise. And in the end, he went to the cross, despising its shame (Hebrews 12:2). He took on a crown of thorns, was whipped, beaten, scorned, mocked, you name it. Jesus died for *all* the sins of the world and, eventually, rose again three days later, defeating death once and for all—just like he said he would.

Think about the connection here. Just as the Israelites were enslaved in Egypt, we were slaves to sin and death. But God didn't leave us there; he sent Jesus to lead us out of bondage and into the promised land of grace.

He stepped into our Egypt, saving us from our exodus and marching us out in freedom.

But that wasn't all. Jesus didn't stay here and continue living. He ascended back into heaven, leaving earth a promise that he would soon return again. He said this:

> Go therefore and make disciples of all the nations, baptizing them in the name of the Father and of the Son and of the Holy Spirit, teaching them to observe all things that I have commanded you; and lo, I am with you always, even to the end of the age. (Matthew 28:19–20)

> And He said to them, "It is not for you to know times or seasons which the Father has put in His own authority. But you shall receive power

> when the Holy Spirit has come upon you; and you shall be witnesses to Me in Jerusalem, and in all Judea and Samaria, and to the end of the earth." Now when He had spoken these things, while they watched, He was taken up, and a cloud received Him out of their sight. (Acts 1:7–9)

Jesus, as he left, *promised* help to be on the way: the Holy Spirit. Now that he died and rose again, we have access to God's Spirit living *inside* us! There's no longer need to carry around God's presence in an ark. He now resides in your *heart*. And when you accept Christ as Lord and Savior, his Spirit is forever with you until the end of the age.

And then, that was it. Jesus left. The disciples were called to carry on in advancing the gospel, led by the Holy Spirit of course. And as the Bible progressively closes, we receive one more promise from Christ that will end everything once and for all: his second return. Scripture promises that Christ will return, finally reigning as king and receiving all glory, honor, and power. His return will not only redeem man but redeem the entire world—God's original plan from the beginning.

And now, we're here. To this present day, nothing has changed. We have been called to take up our cross and follow him, eagerly waiting for him to return, as residents of heaven (Matthew 16:24, Philippians 3:20). That is a short, general storyline of the Bible. God's plan of redemption all along has come true, setting us free by the blood of Christ. Worthy is the Lamb who was slain.

But there's one more thing we need to understand. If you can remember, God gave the Israelites a covenant of commands for them to follow. This is known as the old covenant. But with Jesus, we have been given a *new* covenant, making the old one obsolete (Hebrews 8:13).

The old covenant was law. But the new covenant is abundant grace.

The old covenant was the book of law God gave to his people to provide structure and order within the community. To repeat, it was the *law*. And it gave the regulations on how to be made right with God after a sin, usually consisting of burnt offerings.

But the new covenant's promise is this: Jesus fulfilled the law. He didn't *replace* it. He finished it. Sealed it. Completed it. Because what the law could not do, Jesus already did on the cross. No more need for animal sacrifices and offerings. The Lamb of God is the permanent substitute.

"[God] also made us sufficient as ministers of the new covenant, not of the letter but of the Spirit; for the letter kills, but the Spirit gives life" (2 Corinthians 3:6).

See the power of this difference. There is *no need* any more to try to work your way to God. Jesus is enough. When he shouted, "It is finished" (John 19:28–30), sin and death were conquered once and for all. It's done. There's a new covenant in town and a new way to be made right with God: faith in Jesus. Even when there was no way, God *made* a way for us. He saw us, stuck in our sin, and decided in his own power he would defeat the curse of death and the sting of the grave.

> For what the law could not do in that it was weak through the flesh, God did by sending His own Son in the likeness of sinful flesh, on account of sin: He condemned sin in the flesh. (Romans 8:3)

> Knowing that a man is not justified by the works of the law but by faith in Jesus Christ, even we have believed in Christ Jesus, that we might be justified by faith in Christ and not by the works of the law; for by the works of the law no flesh shall be justified. (Galatians 2:16)

> For such a High Priest was fitting for us, who is holy, harmless, undefiled, separate from sinners, and has become higher than the heavens; who does not need daily, as those high priests,

to offer up sacrifices, first for His own sins and then for the people's, for this He did once for all when He offered up Himself. For the law appoints as high priests men who have weakness, but the word of the oath, which came after the law, appoints the Son who has been perfected forever. (Hebrews 7:26–28)

This is the *goodness* of the gospel in a nutshell. Because we could never be enough, God sent Jesus to be enough *for* us. We no longer have to obey the law to be made right with God; rather, now, we simply need *faith* in Christ, who died in our place! He was the perfect sacrifice and the *only* one who could die for all the sins of the world (Hebrews 10:12). It's done. It's finished. You don't have to be under any obligation anymore to religion. You simply can know Jesus to be made right with God.

It all goes back to the same exact point. It's crystal clear. God doesn't want your *works*. He wants your heart. He made a *way* for you and me to have access to the throne because he desires a relationship with you that much. And as you experience him intimately in this life, it provides further hope for the power and glory to come when he returns.

This entire book was designed to make a bold, radical point. God doesn't desire your efforts. He just wants a deep, intimate, loving relationship with *you*. And through Jesus Christ, we have that ability now because of his death on the cross. That should fire you up! We will walk in glory and experience him throughout all eternity, but God wants to know you *now*.

Don't wait. Don't hold back. Start now. Experience him now. The story of the Bible should pull you toward wanting to know Jesus well and experiencing him deeply. Let your appreciation for what God did ignite a fire in you to seek him even more. Because in the end, his love for you is what will drive you toward him.

Make the move today. You don't have to be religious. You just have to know Jesus. And the good news is, before you were even a thought, he desired this deep, intimate relationship with you. Seek him. Find him. He *promises* to reveal himself to you. Let his love and grace pull you so far that you have nothing else to do but surrender.

He's practically knocking on your door. And all you have to do is let him in.

It's called *abiding*.

"Now he who keeps His commandments abides in Him, and He in him. And by this we know that He abides in us, by the Spirit whom He has given us" (1 John 3:24).

DISCUSSION QUESTIONS

Chapter 1

1) Scripture talks about how we should be affected by our sin to the point of sorrow, deep grief, and extreme remorse (James 4:7–10). Reality is, until we recognize we are in need of saving, we will never fully appreciate the significance of Jesus. In your own walk, how do you view this balance of acknowledging your sin and embracing his grace?

2) How has your distorted view of what God expects from you affected the way you live? Do you see your faith as a relationship, or do you view it as a religious obligation?

3) When referring to your walk with Christ, do you think God values good works and perfection over repentance? Or does he want obedience and love? See Hosea 6:6.

4) After reading the story of Elisha from 2 Kings 6, how has your perspective of God's presence changed?

Chapter 2

1) What are some spiritual disciplines you can start in your own life to build your relationship with Jesus?

2) How has your perspective of what grace actually is changed after reading this chapter?

3) Take a minute and think about your faith walk. Are you trying to impress God with behavior? Do you feel pressure to perform religiously? Or are you trusting Jesus to transform you from the outside in? We have to remember that

he is the one that changes our hearts, and we just have to draw near to him.

4) Do you possess a genuine fear of God? How does believing this principle change the way you live and view God?

5) Just like Peter, we all have been stuck in that situation of sorrow. We did something we didn't want to do, and we return to an old, comfortable place away from God's loving arms. Recall a time in your life where you felt like you let God down and describe how you handled it and moved on. We should always trust that when we sin, he is faithful and just to forgive us (1 John 1:9). Our place of coping should not be in hiding but in resting in the beauty of the cross.

Chapter 3

1) Pain is something we all like to avoid, but reality is, oftentimes, God does a work through the pain, which brings us closer to him. What does the Bible say about trials, and how can we lean on our faith to carry us through tough times?

2) Chances are, you are either going through a storm, just got out of a storm, or about to go through a storm. The life we live always finds a way to provide hardship, but we don't have to live in defeat. How can you change your perspective on trials, and how does your viewpoint of God's goodness affect that?

3) After reading the story of Habakkuk, what was the climax of his faith journey? What decision did he make in his heart that changed his perspective on his circumstance?

4) Just like Paul, sometimes, we can feel victimized and captive to our situations around us. But as we saw in the story, God always has a purpose in whatever we're going through. What circumstance(s) in your life can you find purpose in, even if it feels uncomfortable or uncertain?

Chapter 4

1) What is your joy in the Lord? Take a moment and really evaluate why God is good to you. Maybe even write it down in a prayer journal or notebook.

2) Your life is always moving in the direction of your strongest thoughts. How have your thoughts affected the way you live in the past, and what scriptures do you need to recite/memorize to change the pattern of your thinking?

3) As followers of Jesus, we are called to take up our cross and follow him (Matthew 16:24–25). Make a list of things in your life that you have fully committed to surrender to the Lord. Identify certain things in your life that you still may be holding on to and think about what you can do to better understand how to give it completely to God.

4) Whose story does your life tell? In everything you do, who are you representing? Does your life reflect the truth of John 3:30, "He must increase, and I must decrease?"

5) Think about the reasons why you go to God when you do. Sometimes, we get so caught up in what God can do for us that we forget what he has already done—provided salvation through Christ Jesus. Is his grace enough for you? Or do you need something extra to be satisfied?

Chapter 5

1) John 14:6 tells us that Jesus is "the way, the truth, and the life." After reading this first section, how can we, as followers of Jesus, replicate these principles he lived out in our own lives?

2) Just like Isaiah, when we come to moments of genuine repentance and restoration, naturally, we receive this overwhelming desire to share it with others. Have you experienced this abundant joy? Recall a moment in your life where God's faithfulness and mercies were evident. How can that relate into discipleship?

3) Sometimes, we get so caught up in good works in the future that we forget to submit and honor God today. Remember, you aren't called to a work—you're called to a revival. What are some day-to-day things you can do for God, right where you are?

4) When dealing with other people, we have to replicate what Jesus is full of: grace and truth. In your own life, where are some areas that you need to treat people with more grace? Where are some areas where you need to treat people with more truth? How do you balance both?

Chapter 6

1) On a day-to-day basis, how much do you think about eternity? Colossians 3:2 tells us, "Set your mind on things above, not on things of earth." Reality is, what we believe about eternity determines how we choose to live today. Evaluate your thoughts, motives, and choices and determine whether they point more toward this life or eternal life.

2) Recall the big question presented in this chapter: What matters most to you? How does prioritizing intimacy with Christ affect everything else you do in life?

3) So many people today think heaven is somewhere we just end up, but reality is, for Christians, heaven is home. How has your perception of heaven changed after reading this chapter?

4) Remember, when we trust the Spirit to transform us, only then will we begin to see our hearts change and our motives point toward Christ. What role does the Holy Spirit play in our own process of sanctification?

5) After reading this book and reflecting on these questions, I hope this point has been made loud and clear: Jesus is offering you so much more. There is abundant life with him at the forefront and freedom because of the cross and the empty tomb. How has this book affected the way you view your relationship with Jesus? What is your next step to finding true, abundant life found in Christ?

ABOUT THE AUTHOR

Ryan Shieh is an author and student athlete at Liberty University in the 2025 graduating class. Ryan currently plays on the baseball team at Liberty and is pursuing a degree in pastoral leadership, wanting, one day, to lead a church. Ryan has been writing books about his faith since 2020, with his most recent one, Restart: Finding Your Purpose through Christ. His hope and passion consist of showing others the love of Jesus and furthering his work in the hearts of people all over the world. Ryan aims to one day start a foundation for kids in need of physical resources and, also, sharing the gospel story.

Lightning Source UK Ltd.
Milton Keynes UK
UKHW022241310123
416265UK00005B/296